Break Free from Fear and Doubt

WIN@LIFE
Entrepreneurs

Lessons, Steps, Tools & More.

By Wayne Walsh

ISBN: 0692128425
ISBN-13: 978-0692128428

DEDICATION

This book is dedicated to my parents Douglas and Negretta Walsh. Thank you for working so hard to provide a life for all of your kids. We appreciate what you did and it set the foundation for us to do whatever we believed we could do in life. Love, Wayne.

CONTENTS

WIN AT LIFE – FOUNDATIONS AND LESSONS

When adversities and obstacles come our way, we have a few choices. We can either attach ourselves in a negative way to these obstacles or we can step up to the challenge and tackle them. Adversity and obstacles are comprised of energy working against you not with you. This energy is all around you and lies within the hearts, minds and words of others. It lies in the actions, glances and chance happenings around us. What we must do when this energy seemingly moves against us is to use the energy in a positive way to get things done. First on the list of getting things done should be to tackle those obstacles and the adversity, changing things in your favor. Or better yet, elevate your mind and reality to a point where there are no "obstacles".

This is something I just so happen to be currently doing writing this book. At this very moment, my wife is pregnant with our twins and has spent the day in the hospital. I took care of our 16-month year old, who was very demanding of attention, especially since her mom wasn't around. Then when we picked her mom up from the hospital, my daughter was extra fussy that mom couldn't pick her up and play with her. It was an exhausting day for everyone. After my daughter and wife went to bed, I took whatever fatigue and frustration from the day and turned it into a positive force to change my attitude and reality. As a matter of fact, the noisy neighbor next door watching their movie extra loud on what may be movie night is extra motivation to see past any negative obstacles and through any reality that I don't wish to last. Ultimately, I must take responsibility for my reality. That's the only way that I can change it.

At the same time, even though obstacles are forces that stand in our way and work against us, sometimes we need them for us to GROW. Obstacles present challenges that can allow us to be the best version of ourselves in overcoming whatever is in our way.

Personal History

I've lived in the inner city, city, county, suburbs, even on the beach, all as a boy and young man. I've attended private, catholic, and public schools, taking public transportation until about 23 when I finally went for my driver's license. Many pivotal moments standout including many great family moments, inspirational and motivational moments, including at church and throughout life in general. I had an awesome and very enjoyable sports career that included track and field, soccer, and basketball.

Growing up in the inner city of Baltimore, we felt blessed to be so close to the Inner Harbor. We would run there every morning with our father who loved to run and ran track in college. The views of the city were so beautiful, with people of so many races and cultures living next to each other in one big community. The police were community oriented, knew the residents and lived among us too. We lived near Patterson Park and Fayette Street which my classmates in high-school dubbed the "jungle" because of the craziness that was going on there. Before assuming that title of the jungle, it was home, until around the late 80's when drugs hit everywhere hard but especially the inner city. That's when we started to see drug busts, hear gunshots, see robberies, etc. Unfortunately, as residents it seemed to be the way of the world and we carried on with our lives.

Our parents always placed a heavy emphasis on education, so even while living in the inner city, we went to one of the best private schools in Baltimore, Grace and St. Peters. They provided a powerful curriculum that included travelling throughout Baltimore during the day to local community pillars, like the Maryland Historical Society, where we learned about history and grew a love, interest and curiosity for history in general. We visited the YWCA, where we learned to swim. Then there was the Meyerhoff, with its display of classical music, The Lyric and Center Stage with their plays and shows. The City was and still is rich in culture and class.

I was able to learn the fundamentals of life from great parents who immigrated here from the Caribbean and brought with them basic, yet timeless values, ethics and morals that as children we would use as the compass for the rest of our lives. There were basic etiquette, organization and cleaning routines they taught us that proved invaluable in life. Before the age of 10, I had travelled to the Caribbean and seen pristine beaches with white sand and blue waters. We tasted jerk chicken and coconut from the side of the road, as was customary and danced the night away to reggae tunes at an Ocho Rios Resort.

Early Wins

Sports

What it took for me to become a champion can be used in other aspects of life too.

Passion and Love

If you want to be the best, make sure you have passion for what you're doing. You can have an interest in doing something but having passion is going a few steps further and having a genuine deep-rooted interest that doesn't waver. You're constantly focusing on that passion and how to improve. I had an early passion in sports, whether it was soccer, basketball or track and field and that translated into winning with my teammates. We loved what we were doing and didn't want to be doing anything else at the moment when we were engaged in the game. We were totally tuned in mentally and gave 110%. We loved what we were doing and studied the greats that were playing the sport too, practicing their moves and trying to develop our own.

Practice

To be the best and win championships in sports or in life takes practice. I can remember getting up early and practicing basketball or track when it wasn't even mandatory. I would either individually or with a couple of team members practice at 5 or 6 o'clock in the morning before school started. Whatever your passion in life, apply that same work ethic and if you truly love it, it's worth getting up early to work at it. I remember for basketball I didn't even have a hoop to practice shooting. What I did have was a driveway so I made sure whether I could shoot or not, I would definitely be one of the best dribblers out there. Sometimes you have to be resourceful and work with what you have until you can get what you want. I was still able to play at the local recreation center after school or at the neighborhood basketball courts. This is a reminder that sometimes you have to schedule when and where you practice as well. If you can't do everything where you live, then plan to practice certain things elsewhere.

Competitive Nature and Will to Win

Growing up in a big family with 2 brothers and 2 sisters, competition was constant and something used daily. This naturally carried over when playing with friends on the playground at school or at the neighborhood park. Life is also competitive and you can't let others crush your dreams; instead have a will to win like some of the great sports competitors. If you love what you're doing and practice at it, then being competitive is a natural progression. In order to back up your competitive nature, you have to put in the work so you're actually good and excel.

Church

Structure

As a kid growing up in the church, I served in pretty much every position you could serve in without being an ordained minister or deacon. This included carrying the banner, cross, torches and of course singing in the choir. This also included reading lessons in front of the church, participating in the annual Christmas pageant, singing one of the Three Kings verses. You name it and as kids growing up in the church we participated in the different facets of the church. Whether we realized it at the time or not, this showed us that each role has its own set of responsibilities and relies on the other roles. In addition to sports, we saw at church how a team operates to accomplish a goal. The goal in church was a seamless ceremony and each role was integral and connected to the others. Also, we were challenged to take more and more responsibility. If you mastered one role, you would move on to the next, etc. It's the same thing at a company where you first master your role and then have the opportunity to take on another one with increasing responsibility. Sometimes you have to be keen enough to know whether or not there is truly room for advancement in a position as well or if your company is comfortable keeping you where you are.

Punctual/Time

Service always started on time as well because hundreds of people arrived at church with 1 designated start time in mind. You couldn't arrive at 11:15 for a service that started at 11 o'clock because the service would have started without you. We would try to show up 30 minutes in advance and you can use that lesson in your personal, business and/or professional life. Why not get there earlier to account for what could go wrong so that you have time to adapt as needed?

Singing in the choir was all about time in a different way. You have to understand the notes, the timing of the notes and how each singer fits together to produce the beautiful music. You had your bass singers, tenors, sopranos and they all had different parts or the same parts and different notes.

Faith

We were fortunate having parents, a church and a school early on that helped us to cultivate faith. It's not the easiest thing in the world believing in the unseen but that was the gift we were given at a young age. Our perspective was always shaped by knowing there is a higher power and a powerful story behind it all too. This directly crossed over to every part of my life and was a critical element when I started my businesses. As entrepreneurs we have to believe in the unseen, that one day we can build a company and/or create a product that will add value to people's lives. That's the whole point of life right, creating something every day. When you live, you inevitably create moments every day. An entrepreneur will deliberately try and create a series of moments that can lead to a desired outcome. Obviously, not just entrepreneurs do this but anyone with professional or personal goals. It helps knowing there's a higher power with unlimited ability who created the earth you walk on. You were made in his image so no doubt you have inner power as well to create, overcome, forge ahead and achieve success.

Community

Growing up, the city was all about family and community. Everyone understood that the output of the community was a direct result of the effort of individuals, families and groups. People took pride in the appearance of their house and you would always see someone sweeping/cleaning their stoop. We were taught to be respectful of elders and we were. My brothers and I rode our bikes throughout the neighborhood and had a comfort level with our community. We also went to the recreation center and enrolled in some of the programs there. Of course, we also went running with pops down to the Inner Harbor as well on many mornings. Police lived among us and were community cops, who knew and communicated with residents, who were in turn respectful as well. Drugs changed many cities across America in the mid to late eighties. I think there's a few lessons here including keep drugs out of your circle, nothing good comes from it. Yes, I'm talking about using drugs, don't do it, keep a clear mind, body and soul to utilize your maximum power. Another takeaway is in building your entrepreneurial community, you can't be afraid of individuals but instead explore and communicate with them. Also, a community is made up of like-minded individuals with a common goal. Whether the goal is to have a high quality of life or to grow businesses, the power of communities with a clear trajectory is special. I saw when drugs killed that trajectory so don't let either the literal or metaphorical drugs do that to you.

Culture

Culture is powerful and growing up, we saw in the city a vibrant culture of history, arts, including music, sports, and more. The Inner Harbor was being built into what it is today with the Science Center and National Aquarium. There was the Maryland Historical Society, Zoo, Meyerhoff (symphony), Baltimore Arena, Recreation Centers and more. These entities all coalesced to make for a powerful cultural experience. You also had annual events like Artscape and the African American Heritage Festival.

Celebration

We lived in the city and my parents believed in investing in education so we always went to good schools whether that meant private, catholic or public. Instead of cable tv, the latest clothes, sneakers and video games, our parents decided to invest in knowledge. They also realized that life experiences were precious and made sure we celebrated every holiday, birthday and other celebrations. They also made sure we went on vacations that expanded our world and introduced us to our heritage. My parents are from the Caribbean and that was a favorite destination. I remember travelling to Jamaica and staying with family where there might not have been AC or cable tv but the food and company was amazing.

We would travel through Kingston to visit family, stopping on the side of the road for 2 things, either jerk chicken or green coconut. The farmer would chop the top of the coconut off with a machete for you to drink out of the top. Once you were finished drinking the coconut water, you would then open the coconut and eat the jelly. We even stayed a few nights in Ocho Rios and on the beach saw water that was so clear you could see right to the bottom. There were orange jelly fish, stingray and fish galore. We would end the night by hanging out at a family friendly reggae and calypso party, dancing the night away. Even at 8 years old, I knew these were special times. It's important to dance, laugh and enjoy life. Celebrate life whenever you can. Make an excuse!

Life was good but still had its challenging moments and life altering ones as well.

Pivotal Moments

Growing up in our family, you either had to play sports or participate in another extracurricular activity after school. So most of my life, I decided to play a sport after school. There was a period of time in like second and third grade where I sang on the choir. Besides that, I played soccer, basketball, cross country and track and field. I was always the fastest kid on the playground and when I started high school, took that speed and joined the basketball team. Soon after, I was scouted and recruited by the track and field coach, joined that team and had great success. Most of my life, I thought that I would be playing a sport professionally. I had won team championships from soccer and basketball while in Catholic school to the state championship in track and field while in high school. Things progressed so well that for the city championships in my senior year, I had scouts from colleges all throughout Maryland coming to take a look at me.

Sometimes life has a way of throwing a curveball that you would never expect and that's exactly what happened here. One day, we had a national fitness test in gym class and being the self-proclaimed fastest kid on the playground/ in school, I just had to do my best here. Or did I? Nevertheless, as I was competing in the national fitness test, I hurt myself. This injury would cause me to limp around the track at the City Championships and ultimately miss out on a track and field scholarship and a glorious ending to my track career.

Fast-forward about eight years after that, I was introduced to the world of entrepreneurship and found my next passion in life. However, the time in between was spent searching for what that next passion would be since sports was really all I knew. This is why one of the types I clients we look forward to working with are athletes or ex athletes looking to make the transition into business because we understand what a shock it can be. Imagine thinking that you're going to be fulfilling a dream for a certain period of time and that's cut dramatically short. You're faced with the stark question of what other dreams do you have? Luckily for me I found that dream in the powerful form of entrepreneurship.

I went on a personal, mental and physical journey that would allow me to be a fearless entrepreneur and father. I'll show you how I got there and share steps on how you can start or grow your business at any stage in your career, business or life by using guiding lessons, steps and tools. Enjoy!

The book contains fundamental lessons learned early on in life and reinforced throughout. If you want to know how I went

From:

- Preparing for City Track Championships where scouts were coming to see me run to determine my college scholarship qualifications.
- Getting hurt in gym class of all places and not being able to perform in the City Championships. Dream of College sports and Olympics temporarily crushed.
- No clear path or goals

To:
- Clear Path and Goals
- Journey
    o Moving to South Beach
    o Starting my first business
    o Finding Love
    o Graduating with an MBA, specializing in entrepreneurship
    o Getting Married
    o Having my first child – A girl
    o Leaving my job
    o Starting my third business/ A profitable successful venture
- Growing as a citizen, man, husband, father and son.

The Awakening

I know the title sounds like a horror flick but my awakening was far from that. It's important to say that how we awaken and the journey after is different for each of us. For me, my purpose wasn't clear and part of that was just being young. I always had faith in the Lord and Savior Jesus Christ. I always knew that things would work out. He was my protection, he was my shield. I also had good instincts and along the way both guided me to where I am today.

Lesson: <u>Know your strengths. Know what pulls you out of situations</u>.

The sooner you know, the sooner you can lean on those strengths.

So what is awakening? Well, it's awakening to your life's purpose. Awakening to your truth and what SHOULD be your reality.

My instincts guided me from situation to situation. My faith did as well and let me know things would work out. In fact, my instinct was a reflection of my faith. So I simply allowed God to work through me.

<u>What I Learned about Possibilities by being cast for an HBO Movie – 3 Steps</u>

When I was around 23 and still figuring things out in life, I started on a journey to find myself and answers. I talk a lot about the journey and lessons in Win at Life. After learning new lessons and having existing ones reinforced, I started having conversations with people. These conversations were about people not necessarily believing or agreeing with these same lessons.

They might say "Yeah, the law of attraction is great and everything bro but you have to pay the bills right. That's the reality and just thinking about getting rich isn't going to make us rich". Then I'd say yeah but the first step is you must visualize and see the dream, then you can make it come true. I'd have these conversations with different people and I found there were more that didn't *really* believe in faith being able to influence action and results.

While still on my journey, I decided to conduct a real-life test. Now maybe in New York City or L.A. this test might seem easy and not really proving anything. However, being from Baltimore and not in a film or T.V. group of friends or associates, I knew the test would be a stretch and prove something. First, I guess I should tell you exactly what the test was.
Everyone growing up plays around with the idea of being an actor, athlete or singer. I simply chose one and went for it. I decided I was going to try to be in a movie with no formal training, experience or contacts in the industry.

<u>Step 1</u>

First, I had to believe it was possible, that's it. I'm sure a lot of actors will tell you, before anyone believes in you, you'll have to believe in yourself because there are tons of actors. Same as in business, there are tons of businesses, but as an entrepreneur or CEO, you need to know and feel that your business is special and destined for success.

For me, I had history to lean on, in my own personal journey where I saw that dedication in sports lead to winning and championships in basketball, soccer and track & field. Also, at a young age, I saw so many parts of life from the concrete inner city to lush Caribbean islands, that I truly knew anything was possible.

Step 2

After checking my belief, I had to then seek out how to accomplish this goal. So next, I sought out information. I did 2 things specifically. I spoke to my brother who went to school for film and gathered as much information about the industry, opportunities and possibilities in general.
Next, I joined an actor's newsletter for free and started tracking any opportunities. The first opportunity that I thought could be valuable was an event for actors. I thought it was a perfect event to attend to talk with others about their experiences and find out if they knew about any opportunities.

Similar to getting a job or landing a new client, I knew finding an opportunity in acting was going to involve talking with people in person. Isn't film ultimately about networking, talking and generally connecting with people? Not only telling a story but connecting with the audience. I was able to do both at the event, tell my story and listen to others, ultimately connecting and getting a better idea of what it takes to make it in the industry.

Step 3

I found out a few things during those initial 2 steps that led me to being cast as an extra in an HBO film. One thing I found out was there was a major player in the Baltimore area that did all the casting for the show, *The Wire*. The second thing I found out was that headshots were very important and I needed to get one. I actually went to the mall and purchased a headshot from a photo studio for like $15 bucks. I then mailed the headshot in along with my acting resume on the back. Now you'll remember I didn't have acting experience so this is where I was creative. My creativity must have paid off because I was selected as an extra to receive $100 a day for limited work but it proved the initial test. I received my $100, took my photo with Gabrielle Union and Mos Def and later watched Something the Lord Made on HBO, with absolutely no scenes with me in it. Even though I didn't make the final cut, that experience just reinforced my belief that anything was possible. With that test complete, it was time to start moving....literally!

Lesson: It's important to always be thankful for life's blessings but you don't have to be satisfied.

You shouldn't be satisfied especially if it isn't a true and robust reflection of your life's purpose.

START

To this day, there's no shortage of recent unemployed college graduates or unhappy working professionals. I was both and after my life of being an athlete, I then graduated college and didn't feel like I could find the job I was looking for. Then everything changed, I started looking at my career differently, finding happiness and the ability to get any job I wanted and ultimately success.

Steps:

1. **Assess your own worth and value. Do you think companies are valuing your knowledge, experience, skills and offering the positions and compensation you desire?**

I thought that companies were not valuing my education or experience. As a recent college graduate at the time, I had attained a Bachelor's Degree in Communication. Also as a 23-year-old at the time, I had seven years of customer service experience from working in retail sales including work in the financial services industry. In the financial services industry, I cold called potential clients about the company's products. As a college student, I worked at the Campus Recreation Center for five years in an operational and customer service capacity as well. I even spent some summers working in an operational capacity for Orientation Services, the department responsible for preparing for the arrival of new students on campus. Another summer , I was also the Head Tutor Counselor for a pre-college program. You take all of this experience along with my college degree and after graduation it was still tough to get a job. I'm sure you all can relate which is why you're reading this book now.

2. **Tap into your willingness to make a change. Are you willing to shake things up a bit to get where you want to go? What are you most fearful of and what's a possible plan of action?**

I tapped into my willingness to make a change and shake things up a bit. After thinking deeply about my future, I didn't really see any other way but to make a dramatic change. I did find a great job after graduation and gained more experience in business operations, project management and planning. I was even able to buy a car but honestly this was only because I was still living in my parents basement. The sooner I became honest with myself on that reality, the sooner I could set sail with a new plan. The reality of the situation was that the job didn't pay enough for me to live on my own and the prospect for pay or position advancement within the company was nonexistent. Sometimes our job experiences are for just that, the experience. I decided to use my experience and take a chance.

3. **Make a list of all those distractions in your life. Do you think you could eliminate them or greatly reduce them?**

I decided to move to Miami Florida and it was here where I was introduced to entrepreneurship. I saw this wealth and success and simply started reading, researching and flat out asking people what they did for a living. One of the biggest consistencies amongst those with wealth was entrepreneurship and investment. I started my first business while in Florida but realized I was still unfocused and needed to totally block out all distractions for me to be a success. For me those distractions were watching tv and partying including drinking. I decided to move back to Maryland, enroll in an MBA program, eliminate watching tv and partying and add reading, working out and education.

Distraction is such an easy thing not only for college students but everyone because focus reveals reality. If the reality is you're not happy with a job or have any idea of what you want to do in life, then the perpetual question is why not just watch tv, go out with friends, relax and generally enjoy life. While that's important to do for balance, that can't be all you do right? For true enjoyment deep down to our soul/core, there must be more. We're spiritual beings and while working or going to school is great, being a great friend and family member is great, there's usually that other thing you can't quite put your finger on that's missing. That thing that you're kind of interested in or passionate about but haven't started yet. Or there's that feeling that you don't even know what you want to do or where your passions lie. The latter is even more dangerous because idle hands will find activities that aren't always beneficial to the owners' future. My journey was about finding this passion and life purpose, something that many people go through every day. Still my journey was unique and I think there's something of tremendous value to share from it and know you will too.

Move When You're Feeling Stuck

Using my instincts (reflection of faith), I moved to Miami. The solution usually is to move, it's just that simple and movement can come in a mental, physical, spiritual and geographical capacity. Decision is also key as well. The decision I made when I moved to Miami the first time was to enroll in law school. Even though I didn't end up enrolling, I made the decision to physically and mentally move. As a result of moving, I was introduced to entrepreneurship in Miami. When I was living on South Beach and working in Hollywood Florida, the permeating question was where was all of the money coming from to buy the Rolls Royce's, Ferrari's and Lamborghinis that I was seeing on a daily basis. The other thing that I saw on a daily basis was people struggling to make a living as well. I learned by asking people what they did for a living that the great wealth equalizer was entrepreneurship and investment.

The stark truth is that if you don't start today on the path to uncovering what you want to do or doing what you want to do, time will keep ticking. Never think you're so young or have so much time ahead because the truth is that you don't and must use each precious second, minute and hour. Another thing is don't be afraid to move more than once. The beautiful thing is that you're not a tree and you're more like an architect so you can move and design your life.

Steps:
1. Decide if a short term or longer-term move could help in shifting mindset.

Questions:
1. What aspect of the dream or goal do you feel stuck on specifically?
2. Do you feel that a trip or permanent move could help?

I started my first business while in Miami with a friend and it was more so a fun lifestyle business. We were in music management which was something fun to say in Miami. We had a few artists we worked with and were making no money because I wasn't trying at all. After some reflection, I realized I wasn't trying because I lacked the confidence to grow the business. After digging even deeper, I realized I lacked the basic business knowledge needed and was not motivated enough or resourceful enough at the time to teach myself.

South Beach Life

I'll use South Beach life here as a metaphor for fake fulfillment. No disrespect to South Beach or Miami, this is just a metaphor that fits well once explained. I could say Hollywood life too but South Beach is what I know and am familiar with.

One of the main things I like about Miami is the year-round great weather, white sand beaches, and active lifestyle. It reminds me a little of the islands without actually going there. You have the beautiful water, white sand, plenty of activities and a diverse population from Cuban, Haitian, Jamaican and more. It's a southern melting pot of people, cultures, food and more. The ability for me to run or walk outside year round without worrying about snow, sleet or ice is priceless. Also, some extended family members and good fiends live there so it feels like a second home.

At a time in the early 2000s when Miami was hot, including real estate and events, I lived there right on Collins, a block away from the ocean. I had a job that could pay my rent and bills. I had a car, girlfriend, cash in my pocket and went to happy hours and clubs with my attorney friends. I saw stars on the regular either riding mopeds on the beach or at some exclusive party. Some of the highlights of living on the beach included great weather all the time. Even when it's raining, it doesn't seem to last very long but it does come down hard. With great weather all the time, there's plenty to do in this rich cultural oasis. One of my favorite things to do would be to start on 28th and walk all the way down to First and Ocean and back up to 28th. I can't tell you how many miles it is but I know it was a great work out, stress reliever, and provided time to just think and meditate. Now of course as you get closer to the heart of South Beach and depending on what time of day it is, there could be a whole lot of people and a whole lot going on. The morning on a weekday, during a time where there's no big events going on is surprisingly calm for the locals to just hang out. The beach is beautiful and you can swim and do other activities in the water in addition to attending pool parties and outdoor parties at places like Nikki Beach.

I actually lived in Miami twice, once when I was single and then once after getting married and starting a family. Each time, living in Miami provided an opportunity for me to reset my barometer and direction in life. The first time around I discovered entrepreneurship and started my first business.

The second time around I amplified my faith and confidence during a tragedy allowing me to step away and start The WiseWe company. This is why today we make sure that one of our annual Entrepreneurs Retreat events is in Miami. Entrepreneurs Retreat is all about entrepreneurs, literally retreating, running away from their business and work in order to gain a better perspective with the aid of information, tools, support, inspiration motivation and more. Check our website for more details there.

Great life right? For me, growing up in such a great family, seeing what was possible from a very early age, I had questions. I also had questions after being exposed to so many entrepreneurs, investors and people who did not rely solely on a 9-5.

Super Bowl

I can remember receiving an invitation to the vendor meeting for The Super Bowl. Actually through his network, my partner was able to secure an invite. I'm pretty sure we didn't dress up and definitely didn't arrive at least 30 minutes before the start of the event like I do nowadays. I can remember being intrigued by the event not because there was free food and drinks, rather there was feeling of tremendous opportunity. We were one of the businesses at a meeting to learn how to be a vendor for the Super Bowl, the biggest sporting event every year and that was exciting.

We had just started our business to manage musicians and the fact that there were so many other businesses there selling all kinds of different products and services was amazing. These were regular people who figured out their path and then how to execute and that peaked my curiosity and would light a flame for my passion in entrepreneurship. While networking with these business owners, it became clear that they were taking their own destiny into their hands and trying to make things happen.

One of the biggest things I noticed was the preparation that went into attending the event. People had certain clothes on, business cards, folders explaining their businesses and a 30 second pitch of what their business was all about. More than that, they were prepared to ask specific questions of the Super Bowl Committee. They were actually less focused on the food and drinks and more so on making a connection with either the committee or other businesses. Over the years, I would become more and more prepared for big events like these. It definitely takes preparation, practice and experience to be able to excel at a huge event with so much going on.

Life Changing Questions

- What if I don't have to work a 9-5 to pay my bills?
- What do I really gain from the seemingly endless party life?
- If I am truly a man of faith, what honorable risk am I currently taking?
- Is my life going to always be about a job, money, the beach, parties? Is there freedom in that?

It was truly my exploration of faith and freedom that ultimately led me on a path towards happiness and fulfillment. In my case, it took me living on South Beach, seemingly having everything to figure it out.

Risk Everything

After a lot of prayer, I was divinely inspired and made the decision to risk everything, to be the best me that I could be. This would involve returning to the basic lessons learned from my parents, school and church. This would involve hard knock lessons learned from the street. My journey would also be supported by the lessons learned from the boardroom, having worked for the federal government, state government and private institutions.

The logic behind risking everything was that by reaching our true and full selves, we obtain happiness ALWAYS, purpose and fulfillment. I realized why they say that you could have billions of dollars and not be happy. Faith, family, love, passion, truth, integrity, vision, goals. These were things that I knew would empower me. They had before and there was no greater secret to life than a focus on these things to bring fulfillment, purpose and happiness. They had before as a rising athlete, singer, and son. They would again and this is the journey with some of the important lessons learned along the way.

Lesson: When God talks, Get Sober and Listen

The thing is he's always talking and working through us so it helps to have a clear mind at all times. That's just what I did and decided to move back to Maryland to attain my MBA and learn how to start and grow businesses.
You see alcohol and drugs can cloud the message of the divine. It can cloud instinct (reflections of faith) too. I never excelled as an undergrad in college but God and my instincts were telling me that I was better than my current

situation and could achieve greater things. I was better than the job that I was working in, the money I was making and the basement I was living in.

I took those feelings and challenged myself to not only go back to school but get straight A's. When I made the decision to go back to school, the folks at my job started hating. They made it easy for me to leave because they started pulling me into a negative space where I didn't belong and it was obvious. I was in manual labor and my colleagues and manager didn't want to hear about MBA this or graduate school that. So I left, focused on my MBA and sure enough got those A's.

Grow your Dash

What is your dash? You know that little punctuation mark used sometimes between words, the short line. It's just there, suspended in space between two words that actually mean something and bring life to the page while a dash could stand for a few different things but as a short line doesn't actually verbalize it. Deep right? OK, not yet.

Think of the dash as your flatline of existence. It represents a human being, simply suspended in space. We are in fact living on an earth suspended in space, just fundamentally existing. But it doesn't have to be this way and for some, it's not.

For those who choose to challenge what's possible, to achieve the impossible, working to change their mindset and thereby their reality, the dash can be grown. Grow your dash or you're simply existing from a line to a circle as round as the earth and sun. We were meant to grow our dashes and become illuminating forces of purposeful reality. The earth and the sun certainly have clear purposes. The earth to contain and sustain God's children and the sun to warm and maintain the earth.

What's your purpose? I would submit that our purpose is to grow our dashes and by doing so emit an unbinding energy through the universe so that reality bends and changes to match.

Some have shown throughout history that anything is possible, most notably Jesus Christ who ascended into heaven and then returned to earth. Martin Luther King Jr. worked to change the consciousness of a nation. Gandhi chose peace and this peace disarmed and inspired millions.

Entrepreneurs have understood that without passion and risk, they are but dashes existing on a purposeful earth. Their mission is to grow their dash so that they may be as purposeful as the earth, positively affecting and sustaining others. MLK certainly affected many people in a positive way. Jesus affects many people in a way that transcends time and the belief of many. They each had moments where they chose to grow their dash. We all will be faced with these decisions to grow our dash and can do so in different ways.

My Story Continues

I was at a crossroads and chose a path. I chose growth. I chose intellectual challenge. I chose the possibility of more. I left behind negativity, doubt and the inevitability of failure. I chose success and fulfillment. That's where the hard work began. That's where the hard work began that ultimately brought me to you.

I took my instinct and faith and started to build on top. I had my foundation, so I started to build the house. I started to grow my dash.

Lesson: Know you can do better

Lesson: Be willing to step away from comfort zones and challenge yourself

While obtaining my MBA, specializing in entrepreneurship, I also attained true awareness. I realized that I was controlling the world around me. We each have a world or reality that we live in. Oprah, President Barack Obama and Richard Branson created their own reality, being ultimately responsible for their world. I started to realize this after I employed a sober mind at all times and poured my energies into school and self- improvement.

I wanted to make money, make a living and move back out of my parent's basement. Guess what happened? Well those desires and feelings attracted supporting elements that would help me to make that happen.

It started with me being clear on what I wanted and then starting to address any limiting beliefs that would stand in my way. I had to have a continuing, ongoing conversation with myself. Ultimately, I stopped watching the news, then TV as a whole in order to facilitate this self-conversation and growth.

The Awakening Continues

You need more than a conversation with yourself though and what I started to find were really important books, events, people and important causes.

If you're going to change your mindset and reality, then you're going to need help. Seek and ye shall find. There are many great books including this one that can guide you to the destination of clarity and fulfillment. There are many events and groups as well. The message here is to seek them out and fill your life with as many positive pieces as possible.

Books are basically messengers delivering an impactful story or useful information and messages. Nobody should say, "here read this book and it will solve all of your problems or show you the way" (except the Bible of course). However, there are a few that illuminated my journey so I would share a short list here.

The important point for me to mention is that I found in books some of the most important lessons that I'd discovered through my journey that included prayer, lessons from parents, teachers and mentors. In this regard, good books served as reinforcement of the messages that I not only needed to know but act on. Additionally, new lessons and ways of thinking were learned as well.

No one speaker or book is going to answer all the questions you have about life or business. However, a good book can open the doors to a part of discovery, enlightenment and ultimate success as defined by you.

Some of the books I read were:
- The Secret by Rhonda Byrne and co.
- Think and Grow Rich by Napolean Hill
- The E-Myth Revisited by Michael E. Gerber
- The Heart Aroused by David Whyte
- Start Your Own Business by Rieva Lesonsky
- The Big Idea by Donny Deutsch

The Secret

The Secret was a book that made a big impact worldwide. You've heard the author talk about 2 things. The book was the result of a personal journey she went through. Also, it was inspired and based on teachings and lessons from the Bible. That last point is especially important because you always hear successful people say in business that you don't always need to reinvent the wheel.

By writing *The Secret*, Rhonda Byrne and the authors weren't introducing new ideas. In fact, you can track down something called *The Strangest Secret* by Earl Nightingale 50 years prior. This recording essentially talks about the same Law of Attraction that is central to *The Secret*. It looks at how Faith, Belief and Action can have a tremendous impact towards your Life and Goals.

Earl Nightingale can't even receive credit for these concepts either. You can trace these lessons back through time as you would expect. After all, the Law of Attraction is just 1 of the may Laws of the Universe and we know who created the universe right?

If you're working on clearly defining your passion and generating that idea for a business, The Heart Aroused and The Big Idea are good books to read. They align figuring out your passion and brainstorming a business idea really well. What I like about *Start Your Own Business* by Lesonsky is that it takes the seemingly big idea of starting a business and breaks it down into steps. For anyone interested in starting a business, this book covers a lot that you'll need to know and work on. Once you start that business the *E-Myth* coaches you on how to approach growing that business.

If want a full books summary on these I'm sure its somewhere on the web. What I wanted to share were a few books that either reinforced what I already knew or made an impact on my success journey. Maybe they can do the same for you. Enjoy and let me know your thoughts on these books when you read them.

By the way, don't use any one book as a game plan or action plan for your business or life. They can provide a lot of things like motivation, inspiration, information and more. However, none of them can replace the plans that you create for yourself, business and life.

Lesson Recap

- Know your strengths. Know what pulls you out of situations.
- It's important to always be thankful for life's blessings but you don't have to be satisfied.
- When God talks, get sober and listen.
- Know you can do better.
- Be willing to step away from comfort zones and challenge yourself.

Dream Big. Create the Right Vision

Learning how to start and grow a business was not the entire vision. Honestly, the dream and vision was evolving the more I learned and it got bigger and bigger. There's no reason not to DREAM BIG! Also, when you dream small the problem is you just might achieve it. Why not be honest with yourself and what you really want. That way you can pour all your time and energy into attaining that true goal. To figure this out, engage in quiet time, meditation, whatever you want to call it. If you want to become a singer, start a billion-dollar products company, whatever it is, determine what kind of person you'll need to become to attain the goal. Are there life experiences you need to attain to produce the knowledge and comfort needed to acquire the goal? Then move to another state or country, enroll in school, learn on your own, obtain certifications, take music lessons, book recording studio time. Do what you need to start a serious path towards the goal and this is true for business or life.

There's nothing wrong with a big goal but don't forget to sprinkle in smaller life goals. Sometimes we get tunnel vision with just one goal and forget to just live our life too. This is different than focusing on a niche or one business at a time. I'm talking about learning another language, cooking, dancing, whatever it is you're interested in. You don't want to focus on one major thing for 20 years and do everything else in retirement, right? Remember that in addition to business goals, the rest of life should be included as well. This is not to mention family & friend time and individual activities you enjoy also. You might start to ask is it all possible? Of course! Just focus on quality activities and don't be afraid to plan and use a calendar.

Questions
1. How's the balance at work or in your business? Do you feel you're exploring other things you're interested in besides your main big dreams and goals?
2. List the other interests? What are some thoughts on how to incorporate them into your life?
3. What knowledge, certifications, etc. do you think would help in achieving your dreams and goals?

What I Learned from my Conversation with Ice Cube, Before, During and Years Later

First disclaimer is that Ice Cube is not a buddy of mine and it wasn't a long conversation either. The man didn't even know who I was. However, when you're in the same room as people, even if they are celebrities or people you don't know, you can do what? Communicate and have a conversation. That's what life is about isn't it, connecting with people and venturing outside of a comfort zone, embracing the uncertain. While all of that is true, that wasn't the lesson that I learned but is still important to note.

In 2001, when I was 21 and in college, I was lucky enough to attend the NBA All Star Game. My friend J was an intern with the Washington Wizards and they needed some volunteers to help with the festivities, mainly the All-Star experience that took place for fans and celebrities. We were excited about the experience but I wouldn't say we felt like fans or anything like that. In the late 90s, early 2000s in DC, we regularly saw a lot of musicians and celebrities. However, we knew it would still be a great experience and were excited.

We worked hard but the event had a couple of highlights that I remember. At one point, I was in the VIP area watching part of the All-Star Game festivities on TV with Magic Johnson, David Robinson and I believe Dr. J. After 5 minutes, I realized they were cool and I went back on the main floor. After the experience was over, there was a post All-Star Experience function in Union Station. They cleared out the main level of Union Station and there was an open bar and food of all kinds, from filet mignon to lobster and more.

I met and talked with a handful of celebrities that night including some of the cast from the movie *The Best Man*. Then I met Cube and the first thing out of my mouth was "I'm coming for your spot in Hollywood man". Now this was way before I was an extra in a film and more importantly I didn't have big plans to become an actor. I learned a few things during that conversation and years later as well. I did learn that even though I was young, I was competitive and unafraid.

In the years to come, I would search for what I was willing to follow through on. That search for my true passion was the other thing that I remember about the conversation. Essentially, Ice Cube said let's do it, and wasn't fazed of course. In the years since 2001 he went on to do blockbuster after blockbuster movie.

I saw that passion, perseverance and a clear self-identify could go a long way. You might not call Ice Cube the best actor but he always brings energy and reality to the screen. From my brief conversation with him, I could see that his energy has a lot to do with his passion for the craft of entertainment and a clear sense of identity. I didn't fully understand since Track and Field what that meant for me until I found entrepreneurship.

While the vision of what would become The WiseWe Company became clearer and clearer, life continued. Your vision can become clearer as well from all of the lessons learned during your journey. The more I worked towards the dream, the more life still had much to reveal, show and remind me of important lessons that could help guide me along the entrepreneurial and business journey.

Now that you've sobered up (awakened) figuratively or literally, what do you do with your time? What are some of the lessons you'll pick up along the way?

Time Management - What do you do with that time?

The answer is to build your skills, knowledge and overall experience by following what interests you. Also have a vision of where you want to go, then that will make what you need to learn that much clearer. If you don't have a vision yet, then you could try different careers that interest you. That's what I did. I was interested in working for the federal government and that's exactly what I did, to see if that was a path I wanted to follow. I worked for a leading financial services firm as well to determine whether I wanted to get my series licenses and go deeper into that industry. I did all of this in my early to mid-20s. By the time I was 27, I had an accurate vision of what I wanted to do in life and what I didn't want to do and it came from trying different professions and then being very observant of other people's experiences as well. You don't need to work every job out there to determine what you like. You could also take stock of your abilities and tolerances to determine what it is you don't want to do. Now with all of that said, sometimes in life you'll need to do what you need to do to pay the bills. That doesn't mean you stop trying to achieve wonderful things. You can do both at the same time. Whatever you do, why not make it an interesting and exciting journey, whatever that means to you.

Steps:
1. Write out your vision
2. List companies or industries you'd be interested in working in.

Questions:
1. What knowledge do you think you're lacking? What sources are you planning to gather that information from?
2. Are you a part of any business, social meetups or groups?
3. How many books do you currently read? How many would you like to read on a consistent basis?

While living in Miami, the vision for my life and business was not clear. I was content having a job, living on the beach and partying when and where I wanted. However, I could not envision a future that included the same people and surroundings I had grown accustomed too. I knew there was more, I just didn't know what it was. The psychology of business and life success was the BIGGEST thing that I had to MASTER. A New psychology and physiology would fuel my habits, decisions, and help apply knowledge and experience.

I returned to Baltimore to fulfill the vision that more was possible. That I could be a CEO, affecting positive change at the same time and not just pretending to do so. I returned to accumulate the knowledge/know-how to become a successful business owner and then apply it. I returned to become immersed in the community, to have a positive impact on the city, county and all the above. I started my MBA specializing in entrepreneurship to begin learning the important principles, fundamentals and general information necessary to succeed in business.

Trial and Error

The thing about starting companies is you better be ready to do something with it. The fundamentals are pretty straight forward and something I help select clients with today. Starting a business includes registering the company, obtaining a Tax ID and selecting how the company will file taxes (example: LLCs as an s Corp, etc.). What I didn't do with my first business was to actually market the services. I just thought it was cool to be invited to parties, vendor meetings and meet celebrities in Miami. Part of it was lacking the confidence and the other part was lacking the know-how to connect with those who could use our services. Being self-aware, I knew I needed to gain the confidence and information so I started the journey to attain my MBA. Now, do you have to get an MBA to start a business? No. Does it help? Sure, it mainly helps with confidence knowing that you have mastered the disciplines of finance, accounting, operations, entrepreneurship, etc. You could also just read books if you're an extremely self-disciplined person.

Steps:
1. Write out major professional and educational accomplishments to this point.
2. Create an excel that lists and segments your network.
3. List companies or individuals you'd like to add to your network and why.

There was a program in school called Student Consulting Services where we could provide value to local businesses and be compensated pretty well for it. We worked on marketing, finance, business research & analysis and business plans for these companies. The goal was usually to help the business find a way to become more financial efficient or create a greater impact with their marketing, etc. We forged great relationships and were able to apply the knowledge we were learning in our MBA programs. Since I was specializing in entrepreneurship, my teachers and advisors challenged me to graduate with an actual working business. I was so excited to be able to apply the knowledge I was learning in school to help businesses, that I started a consulting company myself.

I was active in the program at the Entrepreneurship and Opportunity Center (EOC). Jim, the director of the EOC offered some good advice to me when starting my business and that was **A Business Should Make Money**. Simple, yet true and something often overlooked by businesses. Some of the most extreme examples are companies that make no revenue but continue to bring in investment or other capital with no return. For 3 years, I made no money BUT gained valuable experience.

Nonetheless, I went all around Maryland networking and learning at FREE or low cost events and seminars. The result was that I learned even more things I hadn't learned during my MBA program. I also grew a network of fellow entrepreneurs whom I could ask questions and vice versa. Additionally, some potential clients came out of my moving around as well. I started helping clients for free and others under a future percentage agreement. What came out of one of these unique client relationships was a cd released on iTunes and clients to use as a reference and example for potential clients.

Don't Forget to Celebrate

On your road to achieving great things, don't forget to take time to enjoy life with friends and family. I had certainly been pushing to change my life for the better and a celebration was in order. The Walshes joined The Thomas family and went to an Annual Caribbean celebration with this particular year being held in the Ronald Reagan International Building. *Every* Caribbean country had a table where they were providing signature dishes and drinks of their country. It was an all-inclusive event that I was able to attend with my parents and siblings. At the end of a long night, just like many years prior, we were able to dance the night away to a reggae and calypso band.

Even more impressive than that All Star Game years before, the food and drinks were endless and the networking top notch. Just like the Ice Cube encounter or so many others while in college, the lesson is to always be prepared. No doubt the point of this event was to have a great time; however there were also Prime Ministers and government officials from countless Caribbean countries so it was a great networking and business opportunity as well. They were certainly approaching it this way with the point of the event being to raise money for the Tourism organization who produced the event. The larger goal being to boost tourism to these countries. It's good to take breaks and yet my journey continued.....

Before I could really get started and fully grow that business, a larger more established consulting company offered me a job that I couldn't refuse. I looked at it as an opportunity to learn the traditional industry of consulting and went from business owner to Business Analyst overnight. Over the next 2 years I rose to Senior Business Analyst, then Project Manager and finally employee of the year, working on multimillion dollar projects. I accomplished what I set out to do, learning the tools of the trade and was prepared to step out again.

THE JOURNEY CONTINUES

My personal journey has provided the lessons and content of this book. We don't do anything alone so of course I've cited influences that I've read, heard, seen, etc. One famous saying is not to reinvent the wheel so to understand how to be successful, I've read about and studied success too. I've studied other successful millionaires and billionaires to understand the skills, abilities and qualities that they possess and utilize.

The greatest teacher is experience and I learned to organize for success and profits through time spent starting businesses. I was able to go from:

> 1. Breaking even/ making no money and not being able to find clients.

TO:

> 2. Finding clients who didn't have much money to spend.

TO:

> 3. Making lots of money and having lots of clients come to me, making my vision come true.

I guess the third time was the charm for me and there is really no telling how long or short it will take things to click for you. The key is, if it's truly your path, you are passionate and have a vision of the outcomes you want, stick with it. I decided to leave regret behind and fully embrace happiness. To me happiness is being fulfilled everyday living and growing towards what you truly represent and expect out of yourself.

Project management is intertwined with our daily lives, there's no way around it. Most everything has an end goal to it and then a strategy or approach on how to go about attaining the goal. The action items/ tasks break the plan into steps that can lead to accomplishing the goal. Whether we're talking about planning a birthday party, wedding, or passing an exam, you can approach these things through the discipline of project management. First, a strong project starts with a strong vision and then continues into the strategy, goals and action steps.

Vision

As the CEO of your life and business, you must have a clear vision in order to get what you want. This will help to provide clarity to everything else that you'll need to do such as setting up strategies, goals and action steps. At the heart of creating a clear vision is being honest with yourself about where you WANT to see yourself, family and business in the future. If I asked someone on the street what they really wanted, they might initially say, to be a baker and own my own bake shop. Then you keep talking to them and by the end of the conversation you find they actually want to be a professional dancer with Alvin Ailey. YES, you can do more than 1 thing in life but what is the vision, how would those 2 things blend together and why didn't they mention both when asked. That's because for many the vision isn't clear. There's many things that interest us but have we ever taken time to see how they all fit together?

Goal

Vision is tied to OUTCOME aka Result/Goal. Ultimately what do you want and envision for your life and business? Even more important than action steps is the ultimate outcome because you can achieve your outcome aka ultimate goal with *unforeseen* steps as well.

If you're able to achieve your ultimate outcome *without having to complete ALL* of your sub-goals and action steps, then this is a quicker path to achievement. Is each action step necessary to build a certain foundation? If so, you may still want to circle back and complete.

Before my business aspirations really took off, I lacked the action steps and ultimate focus & clarity on one goal. However, it doesn't have to be that way for you after reading this book. You can clearly define not only your ultimate outcome but the action steps to get there.

Action Steps

I always had action steps, but action steps without the correct strategy and goals is a flawed approach. What are the necessary steps on the path to achieving your goal/sub-goals? You will need to break this down into a very detailed plan. If an action step involves other possible action steps, break that down further too.

Strategy in Action

I didn't have a strong strategy pre-Miami. Strategy refers to the question: How are you going to get there? I'm not sure I was even clear on what the THERE was. In that regard, I believe your strategy can be fueled by your personal beliefs and mindset. I believed that the only thing different between me and those CEOs I followed was the know-how/knowledge and it was a barrier that I was determined to overcome. The mind is a delicate machine and I had to be careful what I fed it (garbage in and garbage out). My strategy was to generally eliminate all of those things that would not propel me towards my goals and replace them with those things that would. I:

- Stopped watching the news
- Started surrounding myself with inspiration, motivational and informative literature.
- Started listening primarily to classical music
- Engaged in Meditation and Prayer
- Faced fears of:
  - Being alone
  - Accepted
  - Failing

I didn't look for confirmation from others, knew what I wanted and started to go after it. So, before you get into any advanced planning or organizing techniques at a fundamental level, you must:

- Organize around your mindset/way of seeing or dealing with things/perspective
- Beliefs/Mindset fuels strategy that drives business and personal plan of goal attainment/action

Strategy, Goals and Action Steps are 3 central parts of a success plan that you must define early and often.

Keep a Journal (Planning)

With so many questions to answer in your business and personal life, write it down. You can keep a journal with these important answers and that will only help capture your thoughts and ideas along the way too:

- You can capture your goals and daily reflections here
- You can capture daily business & personal occurrences and reflect on them all including what you could do better the next time
- You can keep a list in your journal of major outcomes you're seeking or even daily action items

Lessons:
- **Read BOOKS** of others who have done what you are trying to do
- Turn your car into a **LIBRARY ON WHEELS** with audio books
- **FEED YOUR MIND** with what is possible AND how you can achieve it

THIS IS IMPORTANT BECAUSE

There are so many commercials, advertisements, television shows, news billboards, signs, etc. telling you subliminally what to do or most importantly WHAT YOU ARE CAPABLE OF DOING on a daily basis, every second from multiple channels (phone, environment, and other people).

YOU MUST DELIBERATELY FEED YOUR PSYCHOLOGY (CONSIOUS AND SUBCONSCIOUS) messages that you CAN DO....YOU CAN ACHIEVE your DREAMS. You can also welcome these messages from people who share how they did it.

I fed my mind with books, audiobooks, and surrounded myself with like-minded individuals. Then, I enrolled in a graduate program and ORGANIZED my life with understanding that PEOPLE matter to my success.

Surround yourself with the right people (NOT negative people, doubters) and structure your life to be positive, motivating and inspiring. Treat your BODY like it's precious because it is. Walk, run, eat well and drink plenty of water. Learn, improve and challenge yourself to be BETTER ALWAYS.

Life doesn't wait for your business to be born, it continues and so do the lessons, challenges and triumphs. As you work on your business and dream, remember a few important things. Time with family, faith and human nature are important to understand and nurture in your personal and business growth phase. From marriage, to fatherhood, marketing and sales, these are important areas to focus on and grow your experience.

Idea /Product

You don't need to reinvent the wheel when creating or improving on your product. Your product doesn't need to be a high-tech software or biotech innovation. It could be a service or simple solution to a challenge or problem you've seen in the marketplace.

As an example, I started 3 service based businesses. The first business was a music management company I started after moving to South Beach. After college, I took a job making 10 bucks an hour and was given an office and Nextel phone. While 15 years ago in 2003 that wasn't a lot of money, I was still able to save money and purchase my first car. In large part, this was because I was living in my parent's basement. This brings a few points to mind, the first being if you can save expenses when growing your business, do it. The other is, I think one strong characteristic of an entrepreneur is to know when to take measured risk and even unmeasured gut based risk. The benefit of the job that I took was it helped me to continue growing my professional skills and introduced me to the concept of project management for the first time. We managed the reservation of available conference rooms and classrooms at a university, including working with the contact and entities involved such as security, catering, audio-visual and more.

A college degree is wonderful but at the end of the day employers are looking for experience too. I came to the realization that to grow, I needed to move so I moved to Miami. After packing up the car, I drove down without a job. Shortly thereafter, I continued my experience with planning events after securing a job. My time in Miami was great. So much wealth was on display that I started asking the question what does everyone do to accumulate this freedom, success and wealth that was on full display. That question led me to the answer of entrepreneurship and starting my first business which was a music management/ consulting company. Over the next 13 years, I would start 2 other consulting companies. The WiseWe Company has been the most successful helping fast-growing companies by being an operational partner. For example, one of the many things we can do is to help leverage Salesforce as a help desk by implementing and managing it for clients. We also offer HR and project management solutions so clients can focus on sales, finance and/or something else. Now we're focusing on how to reach many more people and businesses, so we're creating digital products and group training programs & events. We want to work with you at any time through these on-demand products.

Don't be afraid to seek out FREE expert advice on your idea either, it's a good idea to receive feedback from entrepreneurial experts. When I had an idea, I sought out those experts for free to gain valuable feedback. I visited the state university who was offering office hours on Fridays for local entrepreneurs to come in and share their ideas. I ended up going on several occasions, the first time just to watch and learn about the program itself. The next time I went, I sat down with several of the on-site experts, getting feedback on several of my ideas. This helped me to prioritize which ideas to pursue first and which ones were thought to be great ideas, complex ideas etc. Also what came out of that exchange was information on technology transfer which is the transfer of technology inventions from universities and government entities to the private sector.

Out of this discovery, I scheduled follow-up meetings with the technology transfer office at the University and was able to review and discuss a list of inventions from the university. This is another recommended way to go especially if you don't have an idea of your own. Another discovery that came out of this meeting was an additional free resource called the Maryland Intellectual Property Legal Program. Here, I could set up a meeting to visit with the program director and team to review my ideas. When the idea is accepted into the program, they analyze and offer feedback.

While in the ideation or innovation stage, you can take lessons from a baby…..seriously!

Unlimited Curiosity

Curiosity and happiness can go hand in hand. A baby is always going, always moving. They're full of energy, always looking to be entertained like adults. Adults have cable TV, internet, bars, gyms and more.

Babies love their immediate surroundings which are very new to them, so they continually play with and try to figure out everything around them. Have you ever paid attention to a baby in a bath? They'll play with the faucet, the water, back to the faucet, very entertained with such simple surroundings.

Lesson: Keep it Simple, Stay Exploring.

A colleague of mine shared the experience of interacting with his son who was 8 years old. The interaction he described starts earlier than 8 years old and I could relate to seeing the same in my baby girl.

He told me of an inquisitive little boy who asked him why the leaves were moving on a tree. When his father responded that it was because of the wind, the little boy then asked, what is the wind? Each definition led to a different question and shows how much the young want to learn based on an innate curiosity to make sense of the world around them.

Babies who can't yet talk can discover their world through trial and error. That is how babies learn basic survival skills, including not putting their little fingers in closet doors or trying to stand on an unsteady chair that might tip over.

We should never let go of this basic survival instinct and should nurture it. We should never let go of the curiosity to make sense of the world around us in its simplest elements. This can lead to invention, innovation, happiness, feeling alive and invigorated by the world around us every day.

BREAK FREE FROM THE JOB MENTALITY; FINDING SUCCESS AND FULFILLMENT DOING WORK YOU LOVE

Doing work you love starts out with knowing who exactly you are and what it is you love. You must know yourself first before you can figure out what you truly want and how you can get it.

"Break Free" is really aligned with my story of breaking free from the idea that a 9-5 was the only way to make a living. I've experienced this 3 times having started 3 companies, breaking away mentally a little more and more each time. Part of the secret is that whether you realize it or not, it's a gradual process that occurs until one day, before you know it, you look at work/ a job much differently.

I used to say that my major issue with a job was companies placing a monetary value on you and many times (in a lot of our opinions) that represented a salary that's too low. The thing is even when you start your own business, the marketplace still places a value on your services or product. However, there's a dramatic difference between a job and entrepreneurship. One major difference is that with entrepreneurship there's freedom of choice in what you do. For example, if you sell project management services, a product or whatever it is, that doesn't necessarily mean that you need to be the actual one to perform the work. You can hire employees to perform the work and manage the process, allowing you to have many clients and projects occurring simultaneously. The idea is leverage and the freedom to build a team to create that leverage as opposed to creating a job for yourself. In a job, you have duties but they are your own even if you have a secretary or assistant. In entrepreneurship, you cannot only have a secretary and an assistant but your goal should be to replace your role 100%. The goal of entrepreneurship is not to create a job for yourself but to build an entity that can exist without you.

Do a self-assessment answering questions like:

- What are my strengths and weaknesses? This will show you what you either need to work on or hire for. Hiring a complementary staff in an area where you're weak and clearly delineating everyone's roles and responsibilities would be a smart way to go.
- What are my skills and experience? This will not only help with finding complementary team members and partners. A self-assessment here can also inform what type of business you could build. Some of the easiest businesses to start are those that either involve what you currently do or have done in the past.
- What are my dreams, fears and life philosophy? These elements fuel your vision that we've already discussed. When trying to break free from the job mentality and find work you truly love, you'll want to have a picture of what exactly that is in your head and better yet on paper in a shareable format.

Breaking free from the job mentality involves addressing that mentality head on through conscious and subconscious steps. You can address mentality consciously by reading books, attending conferences and putting what you learn into ACTION.

When you find the work that aligns with who you truly are, it doesn't even seem like work. That's why this is key because who wants to do something that feels like labor every second? You can still work and enjoy it too. There's nothing wrong with work but there's many various kinds so find yours.

Life Philosophy: Master your thoughts, elevate your perspective

You can address mentality subconsciously by these same actions as well as confronting your fundamental beliefs:

- What are your thoughts about a "job" in general
- What are your thoughts as you prepare for and go to work every day?

Your general view regarding a job shouldn't be negative. A job should be a means to an end. To determine the end, you should identify goals, short and long term.

That way, the job can be a stepping stone or motivational tool to get where you want to go. Answering these questions and addressing these issues is a process that begins with building a strong foundation and adding to it. Your foundation includes your general outlook on life, your life philosophy. Some people have a hopeful, positive, energetic philosophy and some don't. Your life philosophy drives the rest of your life so it's important.

Do you blame a lot of your life on what happens in the world, at work or in the economy? Or do you think anything is possible, that there's a lot of positive things in the world and your accomplishments have no limits?

Las Vegas – My Wildest Story Continues to Impact my Business and Life

As The WiseWe Company continued to grow, I was laser focused and not thinking of vacations. We were still a very small company where I was heavily involved with all of the services we were providing our clients. I hadn't yet replaced myself in any of those roles. However; I had the opportunity to go on a pretty cool trip with the family and couldn't pass it up. I remember travelling to Las Vegas and California one winter break and the time zone is of course 3 hours behind. We had a 9am meeting on the east coast which is 6am on the west coast so no one expected me to make the meeting. In fact, up until that point I was told to enjoy my vacation and that they would let our clients know I wouldn't be joining the call. I replied that I wasn't really on vacation and that I would be working on the west coast 5am-1pm every day.

I stuck to that commitment too, right up until Christmas Eve. On the day of the call, I'm up at 3am preparing for the work day (Never really went to sleep I guess). The challenge was looking for a place to have the call. The family was asleep in the hotel room and the lobby area was buzzing, even at 5am because well, it's Vegas. So, I ducked into a hallway and took the call. While my cell phone reception was horrible and no one could hear me, my clients were happy I made the call. Sorry if you thought this story would be raunchy, get your head out of the gutter.

They ended by saying, well we'll be available during the holiday break and we all know distance is no issue for Wayne so even though he's on the west coast, he'll be around as well. That was both great to hear and really the truth about what we stand for which is unwavering passion and commitment to what we do, founded on values and ethics, not money and more money. The root of my approach to my business really comes from this philosophy and mindset. For me, my business is a way of life and clients are extended family so it doesn't feel like a chore or a job, it's more of a commitment to watch over and care for our clients' interests. That's what we've been entrusted with.

Mindset

Philosophy will inspire your mindset and vice versa. One of my favorite books is The Secret because it directly tackles the subject of mindset.
One of the original books to approach it from more of a business and finance level instead of a spiritual one was Think and Grow Rich by Napoleon Hill. Have you read this book?

You will hear "no" many times and have more people that don't believe in you and your idea or your career or life goals especially in the beginning. So, you must believe that you can do it, always thinking positively. At the same time, there's nothing wrong with a dose of reality if you need to switch jobs, your idea is bad or if you should dissolve your business.

Growth vs. Fixed Mindset

Having a growth mindset means that you believe anything is possible and no limits exist. On the other end of the spectrum, a fixed mindset means that a person believes there are limits and boundaries to what can be accomplished and they may even come up with a slew of excuses to justify the belief.

In her book on mindset, Carol Dweck discusses intelligence and talent as fixed for fixed mindset individuals. Fixed mindset individuals focus on documenting talents while growth mindset individuals focusing on growing knowledge and talents to reach undefinable possibilities.

There is a process that we can apply to employ the growth mindset so we are continually evolving instead of stagnant and only reflective. Instead of looking back at what we have become, it is just as important to look ahead towards what we wish to become. Once that vision is clear, dedication, hard work, a plan of action, execution and passion are all components that will carry us through to our best self.

We should strive to be the best version of ourselves that we can possibly be. You don't want to live someone else's life or dreams, do you? I'm sure you don't so it's important to think of growth in terms of personal growth. How you can improve in different areas, what new things you can learn or perceived weaknesses you can overcome?

Shed the Victim Mentality

Victim mentality – Have you ever been called a name because of your race or your gender? How did it make you feel? Why?

Do certain things always seems to happen to you, like money problems, altercations or arguments?

We need to shed the victim mentality by addressing the beliefs that are fueling that mentality of doubt, fear and/or emotional, even physical suppression. We must ask why does someone calling me a name hurt? What do I believe that allows that to happen? If I believe that people in my life are angels, then those who don't act like one don't even exist in my world.

Law of Attraction

Attract the business, job or opportunity you want by knowing and believing. A good book that talks about this is The Secret and the movie by the same name is good as well. Visualize everyday what you want as if you have already received it. You don't have to know how you will achieve but knowing what you want and truly believing you will obtain it, will draw it to you.

If you aren't receiving the money, job or opportunity you want, then there are probably thoughts conscious or subconscious blocking it from coming into your life. The gentleman who wrote the Chicken Soup for the Soul series attracted first $100,000 then $1,000,000 by using this approach and shares the story in the Secret. A classic book that among other things addresses mindset is Think and Grow Rich by Napoleon Hill where he covers The Power of Thought on page 1-17. In these first few pages, Hill tells the story of the man who "thought" his way into a partnership with Thomas Edison, the man who invented the light bulb.

This talk of Mindset and Power of Thought is really a journey you must embark on yourself and can't be covered fully in this book. What I can do is introduce the concept and share books that can guide your journey. The application and use of knowledge translates to power and success. Develop a thirst for knowledge and educate yourself. Arm yourself with the necessary tools to be competitive.

When I changed my mind, my life changed. It takes daily work, down to the second but it's worth it.

Beginning of the WiseWe Company

That's how the WiseWe Company was born. I had a clear, positive life philosophy, growth mindset, no victim mentality and knew that the energy I put out was very important. In 2013, I suffered a personal tragedy that put things in perspective. In my family's worst of times, I still took a positive approach. The message that I received was that life was short so you should be who you truly are.

I wanted to work for a company that would have to fit a lot of criteria and it was a perfect time to build one. With no clients and no money coming in, this situation could have been the perfect storm of total failure and despair. However, with that growth mindset and faith, I knew that things would work out as I started The WiseWe Company in 2013.

I took a night time job as I grew the company. We started by just blogging positive, motivational, and inspirational stories that aligned with our values, ethics and passions. The WiseWe Company was then born. By this time people knew me a little more and attaining clients was a little easier. I had the experience, knowledge, education and team.

When getting started with your business consider offering a trial period for your potential clients. This can be for a low number of hours for an initial 6 months agreement. There's no need to work for free especially if you have academic credentials and some basic experience. Remember that people and businesses have money and your business which offers value is a means of transferring that money from them to you in a trade. When we started the WiseWe Company, we started off with our first big client at 10 hours a week just offering a project management service. Now we provide customer service and project management teams, handling all of the training and HR that comes along with it. This certainly takes a burden off our clients and adds a tremendous value of operational efficiency. Now we're focusing on how to reach many more people and businesses, so we're creating digital products and group training programs & events. We want to be able help you at any time through these on-demand products.

Resources and Tools

You don't have to be in school to learn or receive an education, the Library is FREE. At the same time, you can enroll in school at any age as well and check out books on any topic you desire and immerse yourself in the information. There's a certain amount that you should do each week. There's a minimum amount of productivity that should occur each week and at the very least it should be comparable to others.

What's your song? Music you listen to has an affect not only on your mindset but your life. What is your True North or Life Purpose? Where is your compass set to sail? What is the set of your sail or overall direction and mission in life?

This will inform not only the objective that you will see on your resume but the Vision Statement in a Business Plan. If your story is CLEAR, then you will attract the right job situation, business, or whatever else you're trying to achieve in life.

CLEARLY define your resume objective & job profile (type of job and position you want). CLEARLY define your story, who you are and the skills and knowledge you possess. This is important when making a change with your job or starting a new business.

I started associating with people who shared the same mindset, were on a similar path or even ahead of me. Have a strong team because you can't do everything yourself and can't accomplish greatness alone. It takes great people and a great team.

When I was hired to a brand new federal job, it was through networking. I was referred to a recruiter and that's how I landed the job I wanted. At that federal job, I continued to grow and started to truly believe that I could be a CEO and start my own business. One day when I mentioned this to someone within the agency she laughed. I used that as motivation and shortly thereafter I started my own business and left that job, not working for anyone else for the next 3 years.

Resourcefulness

It's easy to complain about what we don't have or what we want or need. First, we should be thankful for what we have and through that you'll become aware of the resources around you. Like Tony Robbins said to Presidential Candidate Al Gore, it's not a matter of just resources, rather resourcefulness. My definition would be identifying all the obvious and less obvious resources and then actually using them too. It's not enough to simply be aware and it's not enough to know the basics.

Become a resume and cover letter expert. By doing so, you'll define your current skill set and experience level to identify what areas you'd like to grow and learn in. This will also come in handy later down the line when you need to recruit and hire for your business. Then you'll know what to look for, what separates a great resume and candidate from the rest.

We can never stop learning. A major point to life is to continue learning and growing, becoming a better version of yourself. Network to identify opportunities including attending organization meetings like the Chamber of Commerce or other business organization meetings. Write letters, send emails, make phone calls and use social media like LinkedIn. There's a certain amount of measurable progress you should make every week. You can find out who is hiring from family, friends or at networking events. Advertise at these meetings and with people you meet when you're searching for a job. A job is still a good means to an end while growing your business on the side.

To do the work you love, create the experience. Go to the Library and check out Start a Business by Rieva Lesonsky. Attend an SBDC Workshop and obtain a disk of the presentation Start a Business. The SBDC Workshop will walk you through the different elements of the business plan. Also, there are more workshops on different topics. Setting goals aligns mindset and who you are with the right business or even career for you.

- Read page 15 of Lesonsky "Go for The Goal"
- Fill out Personal Goals and Objectives Worksheet
- Things about Me Worksheet
- Does your idea involve something that you're passionate about?
    - o Makes it easier and you're more liable to stick with it
    - o Life and passion don't always get along
    - o Idea should past the test of research
    - o Check uspto.gov for names, copyrights, etc.
    - o Seek legal guidance throughout the process

Life and passion: you must pay the bills in life. You may be working a job you don't particularly like just to get by. Those kinds of things are a part of life and don't have to be a barrier to your ideas and passion.

Make sure to do your research and to check if your idea is out there already. Your local librarian can help guide you in the direction of basic research. Research skills are paramount so you may want to take a class on how to properly research.

Now that I've shared some tools on how to take a new mindset and apply it to work or a new business, let's continue.

Pit Stop on the WiseWe Journey

I took advantage of all the resources that I'm mentioning here and that all led to a job offer with Johns Hopkins. This time I asked, how about hiring my company and not me? The answer wasn't no but it was that it was a process that takes longer and they'd need to consider that. From the research I conducted prior to asking the question, I knew the general checklist they required each company to complete. I knew that process would be much longer than signing on as I did.

That 1 pit stop and opportunity led to our current largest client for The WiseWe Company and a growing team. We could now handle any size client and have all the paperwork on that checklist to win that and any other contract. When our current client approached me, and offered a job, I asked again what about hiring my company. This time I was prepared and signed them as a client.

We also found our sweet spot of service offerings which all companies have a need for. Growing companies with high revenue are seeking to fill a few key positions on a part-time and full-time basis. Instead of hiring directly, another option for companies is connecting with right partner which is what we bring to the table. We're the partner who can fill those positions but then we're also poised to fill others that will naturally materialize as the companies continue to grow.

We can do all the normal consulting work, but really found a niche as a strategic partner offering managed customer service, project management and more. This helps fast growing companies focus on product and sales while we focus on operations. Leading a company and servicing growing companies not only takes mental but physical fortitude. We've covered some of the mental aspects that align with innovation, entrepreneurship, company growth and we'll look at more. For now, let's look at some of the physical aspects that allowed me to work 7 days a week in the beginning, without taking a day off.

BODY IS A TEMPLE – HEALTH, HABITS AND FASHION

When I was either performing at a high-level as an athlete or working non-stop 24 hours a day as an entrepreneur, diet was and still is critical. Diet along with rest and general health is what fuels you on the road to achieving your goals. Consider your diet as you embark on attaining major goals.

Diet

It's no secret that the food you eat is directly connected to your health. With this as a basic fact, doesn't it make sense to pay attention to what you put in your body? Decisions you make about what you eat is partly tied to your philosophy. At a high-level, what this means is that your diet will reflect what you believe about food. If you believe that it's important to put the best in your body for optimal performance, then that belief affects food choices. This must be a philosophy that you believe to your core, as a type of unwavering belief.

Part of designing a diet is making sure there are staple foods that you always keep in your house. Brown rice, whole wheat bread, fruits and vegetables work well for me. Remember an apple a day keeps the doctor away. Nuts, fish, and lean meats like turkey and chicken work well for me too. Find out what works best for your body and plan meals as much as possible. While eating at restaurants is good, making more meals than you buy is probably better. Why? Because you know how you're cooking a meal and what you're putting in it.

You can better ensure the portions and quality of the food is what you want by sourcing and cooking it yourself for the total weekly cost you want to spend. Get with your doctor, a licensed nutritionist and personal trainer to help create your diet. You can have variations on dinner as well and substitute less healthy ingredients for a healthier counterpart.

Exercise

It's also no secret that our bodies require exercise. Yes, all bodies require exercise, a combination of cardiovascular and weight training. As with your diet, you can seek out experts who specialize in design. Dieticians and personal trainers make a living designing and coordinating your diet and exercise routine. Seek them out if needed to design the right one. There are a few key things you can try and do on your own every day.

Walk- We now have technology that we wear on our wrists that counts steps. This is good but I still have a routine of walking at least 30 minutes straight to train the biggest muscle in our body, the heart. Of course, with any workout or diet, consult a physician to make sure your body can handle your daily routine.

Taking the steps is great or walking to the subway or bus is too. In many instances though these activities may take 10 minutes at a time so you still need that sustained cardio activity and preferably several times a day.
In today's world of cubicle office spaces, we need to be as intentional as ever about designing our routine and days. The better designed our days are, the more effective and efficient our bodies can be through exercise and diet. The more effective and efficient our body, the greater the output coming out of it can be, whether that's at work, home or in the community.

People have always commented about how skinny or slim I am and that I don't have to worry about what I eat. In my case, as I'm sure in many others, this is a misconception. Diet and exercise keep me this way so it's really a conscious choice. I believe my physique is built on the foundation of choice and habit. Case in point, when we were pregnant with my daughter, I gained nearly 30 lbs., didn't feel great after the gain and started noticing changes that I didn't like. It was tough running or even walking short distances because along with eating whatever I wanted, I stopped working out as well.

I put myself on a workout routine and diet to lose that 30lbs in 2 months.

I had a good lifestyle foundation to return to which was developed over many, many years. As kids, we would go walking/running to the Inner Harbor a few miles away from our home in Baltimore or in the nearby Patterson Park. Our diet consisted of dinner: rice, lean meats like chicken with the skin cutoff and vegetables. Lunch and snack at school was usually very healthy and filling as well. Our parents made financial decisions that allowed us to attend private school very early on where the meals were great. We never had cable television, expensive sneakers or the latest clothes. In fact, I had hand-me-downs which I was very thankful for. What we did have was a great education and a great family experience. Through this experience, a few things that have worked well for me:

1. Try and run at least a mile a day outside or on the treadmill, preferably the track.
2. Use my bodyweight to exercise and as a measurement tool. This means that there are basic exercises that don't involve weights or machines, but simply our bodyweight. If no machines or weights are required, then why not try and master our own body weight and get in shape at the same time.
   a. Pushups
   b. Situps
   c. Lunges
   d. Planks
   e. Pullups
   f. Dips
   g. Plyometics. Plyometrics is of course something I picked up from track but very useful as far as mixing your running up. It prepares you for running. So, we're talking:
      i. High knees
      ii. Butt kicks
      iii. Twists and Skips

How I Knocked 5 minutes off of my mile time. 10 ways you could improve your mile and get in shape.

1. Start by Believing

Like most people, I run to stay in shape, doing a little every day. Most weeks, I would jog a mile on the treadmill, 3-4 days a week. This is the thing that runners know and you should know. Running on the treadmill as opposed to road or track training is very different. I was feeling good about my treadmill running until I met a marathon runner. You might be saying Wayne, I know plenty of people who run marathons and 5Ks, so what.? Yeah, I know a handful too but when I met a 60-year-old African American marathoner who WON races too, that was much different. I remember talking with him one day and telling him that I used to run track. The question he asked sparked me to start a more challenging journey of running harder with a goal in mind. He said "Wayne, if I can still run, why can't you"? Of course by this. Maurice Pointer meant why I couldn't run harder, competitively and with a goal in mind. Just like that a light went off for me and I realized that if you're reading this and if I was hearing what Maurice was saying, we're still alive so why not aim for the stars. While we're here, we should continue to aim for greatness at any age and in every aspect of our life.

2. Set a Goal to Feel Good About

With new motivation fueling my daily workouts, it was time to set an energizing goal to reach. When setting a goal, set one that you know you can attain with hard work. Don't start by setting the ultimate fastest time that you ever want to run because then you can set yourself up for discouragement. 3 years prior to setting this goal, my daughter had been born and I finished knocking off the 30 pounds that I gained eating pizza, donuts and not exercising. During that process of losing the weight, I ran 8:30 in the mile. As a former sprinter and at 33 years of age at the time, that time was good for me. I remember feeling great and being in great shape so that time represented a great accomplishment.

3. Start the Work

Knowing that I could run faster, improve my fitness while doing it and having a great goal in mind to strive for was just the beginning. The next thing I had to do was start working out of course and as we mentioned in step #1, the treadmill was just not going to cut it when trying to cut down that mile time. The treadmill was great in the winter time to avoid the

48

elements but as March and April rolled around, I knew running outside was the best way to improve my time.

The biggest thing you notice when first running outside as opposed to the treadmill is the environment, especially the air. In February and March in Maryland, it was still cold and a bit of a challenge to run, so I still mixed in some treadmill workouts. For my legs sake, I ran on the track more than the road since it was rubber and a little softer. At first, I kept my workout the same, trying to just run a mile outside as many days as possible. The first mini goal was to run a mile outside comfortably and easily.

4. Keep Track

In February and March when I started with my new running and getting in shape goals, I didn't really keep track that much. I know on the treadmill, I was doing like a 12-13-minute mile. Outside, I really wasn't keeping track, I just wanted to feel comfortable during and after running 4 laps. It took all of February, March and April to do this. As the weather changed, I got stronger and stronger but each workout was hard. On April 14th when I tracked my mile using the Nike+ APP, I was running a 10 minute and 34 second mile already a few minutes knocked off of my treadmill time. Like I said, the miles were hard and I didn't feel like I could run a mile easily until about May. On May 14th when I tracked my mile I ran 9 minute and 33 seconds and could say that I finally felt comfortable, easily running a mile.

5. Hit Your Mini Goal First

To recap, it took around 3 months to start feeling good about running a mile outside. It then took another month to be able to fully run it easily and comfortably. Part of the time it took was probably weather related because on 30 and even 40 degree days, I was not trying to run outside and obviously lost training opportunities. If you live in a warm climate, then maybe you could reach your running goal quicker. Or even if you're a cold weather runner, then the same applies but for me being a summer baby and not able to take the cold as much was a hindrance. Nevertheless, I reached my mini goal.

6. Mix it Up, Up the Miles

To keep the mile easy and make it even easier, I upped the mileage to 2 miles and hit the road. This was grueling but over the course of a month, it made the track mile even easier. By the end of May, I ran an 8:03 mile!!! Something else I did during that month was speed work in the form of

400s. I tried to run as many 400s as possible as close to 1:30 as possible. Yes, I hit my goal and we're only at the 6th step ☺.

7. Speed Works

June was my birthday month and I pushed even harder than the last, focusing more on the speed work, running mainly 400s as well as 800s during a few workouts as well. Yes, I say a few because of what I did in between which is the next step.

8. Rest to Run

To stay injury free, I rested in between workouts usually taking a day, sometimes 2 days to rest. Rest meant making sure to walk, stretch and prop the feet up. What I didn't do but would probably recommend is some kind of icing regimen. See your personal trainer or physical therapist for details on that.

9. Set Another Goal

Even though I hit my goal by the 6th step, I was feeling good and still running. While you have a mini goal that you could set and a main goal, be ready to set another goal once the first is reached. I just wanted to run in the 7-minute realm. When I ran 7:50 on my birthday, I felt really good.

10. Cross Training and Keep Running

There's CrossFit and fitness classes and you shouldn't be afraid to mix it up and try them out. This helped me to keep running when I got shin splints. The next goal was staying in the peak fitness state that I had reached. I visited my doctor for a physical and I even had a peak marathoner's blood pressure.

Try putting on a jogging suit at a major business networking event or interview and see what happens. It's not always about what you feel like wearing, sometimes it's about professional etiquette. That's why this next session is important. It's also important as you craft your personal brand and maintain a reasonable budget at the same time.

Clean Clothing is Important

Why would I include a section about clothing? Well, day in and day out, this is what you're covering your naked body with to go outside, to work, shopping, etc. I'm sure you would agree that it matters just a little, right? You would probably also agree that your clothes should be cleaned and pressed, right?

On your road to being the best version of yourself and creating your experience too, it's helpful to know how to do as much as possible for yourself. This means setting yourself up to be less reliant on others for your success. Ultimately, you should take responsibility for everything in your life. Not that everything is your fault or anything like that. However, by taking 100% responsibility, you'll be able to better control your circumstances.

I've heard many people recommend hiring people to do your laundry. That you can use the time you save doing laundry to make your millions. There are even services now where you can have a personal shopper send you outfits in the mail at a marked-up price of course. I would say that while trying to grow yourself and your business, keep the costs down wherever possible. You don't wash or dry your own clothes, the washing machine and dryer does. Now if you don't have a washer machine and dryer in your home and you must physically travel to the laundromat, then yes, you may want to consider outsourcing that activity. You may want to at the very least choose to dry clean those important business garments, especially the ones that read "Dry Clean Only". I like to use organic drycleaners (no perc) only so you may want to look into that as well. However, if you own a washer and dryer, throw your clothes in, it takes 60 seconds.

Classic Not Trendy

I would recommend to go classic, not trendy when buying clothes. Trends come and go, so your budget would have to keep up with that. Identify certain clothing articles that are timeless and don't change, making them the centerpiece or foundation of your wardrobe. This works if you're a kid going to school or a young or older adult in the workplace and/or raising a family.

Taking your analysis a step further, maybe there are certain brands that are consistent with the look you're looking for and fit your budget. Brand only becomes important when you're talking about quality, budget, symbolism or what the clothing represents. For example look at the history behind Brooks Brothers where Ralph Lauren (Polo) worked and learned about crafting clothes before leaving and starting his own thing. Look at the craftsmanship, quality and timeless look.

What's the Point?

The whole point in talking about things like diet, hygiene or clothing in this book is to get across the following point. Before you take time building a business or forging a loving relationship that leads to a family, what is your personal foundation? Is what you stand for a foundation that can be built upon? Are there lessons that can be passed down to your children or that your spouse or employees will relate to?

Will these be qualities that you'll look for in your employees or spouse, either consciously or unconsciously? Spend some time with yourself to find out what it is you like and don't like, believe in and don't believe in. Not to say that you should force anyone you meet or kids you raise into a box but at least you'll have a perspective. This could help when it comes to offering advice to your kids or enacting a policy or procedure in the workplace.

Good Hygiene

If you're going to stay healthy, then it will be important to clean your hands and body to wash away bacteria and germs. I believe that you should take a shower or bath everyday not only to have a clean body but to wash the bad spirits or energy away. What do you believe?

I also believe you should wash hands before each meal (NOT JUST SANITIZE). Yes, suds up the hands for 30 seconds and then rinse is the protocol.

If you're a man and use a public bathroom, do you use a paper towel when touching the soap dispenser or water faucet? If not, then would you agree that you're sharing germs with every other man that finished handling business at the urinal that day and then touched the faucet or soap dispenser. Dude, just use a paper towel or toilet tissue to touch.

Make a Habit

Etiquette

Some things are viewed as old school when they shouldn't be. They should be timeless values in my opinions.
- Hold door for people
- When walking down the sidewalk, your lady or child walks on the inside of you
- Pull out chair for lady
- Cover your nose and mouth when coughing

You may be reading this and shaking your head in agreement but many people do not do these things anymore, especially the last bullet point.

You have a basic set of lessons, rules, guidelines, etc. that govern the way you carry yourself in life. Some affect you unconsciously having learned them at an early age from your parents, at school or church. For example, I learned to wash my hands before each meal from my parents. I learned most things from my parents like how to wash, cook, clean, basic manners and etiquette like saying please and thank you.

That's another thing that's rarer than it should be, saying please and thank you. For some, it's a laborious chore to either remember to say it or say it at all. It's basic and should be effortless, so if it isn't effortless, examine why and try to fix that one. Don't tell your kids to say please and thank you when you don't. Hypocrites have never been in style.

Abundant Life Blueprint

From dusk to dawn, these are the days of our lives that can be joy filled or filled with negativity.

Morning

How do you start your day? You should be aware of how you generally want to start each day because it matters. If you start the day with feelings of fatigue and dread for needing to get up and out, stop. I know it's easier said than done but you must start changing the internal dialogue that you have with yourself in the mornings.

If you dread getting up in the morning because you dread needing to go to work, then look at it another way. The job you don't like that much is a test to see if you can simply make it there on time and leave when you're supposed too. Simple, right? Think about it as preparation for your dream job and role. You must master some basics first and if you can master them in a position you really don't care for then you're in good shape.

First, I would say identify the reason why you dread getting up. If you say that you're just not a morning person, that limiting belief is then reinforced by those feelings you have in the morning. Through physical and mental conditioning, you can get up and out in the morning in a good way. Look at it another way and perhaps as I looked at it. As my mother likes to say, this too shall pass. If I truly wasn't happy with a work situation, then I would keep in mind that it wasn't going to last forever and it is just what I must do now to get one step closer to changing my reality.

We are in our current realities for a reason. Find out why you are and you will be one step closer to changing it into what you really want. When I worked for the federal government as a contractor, I had to not only commute two hours from Baltimore to DC but get there in a timely manner. Instead of giving negative feelings to this commute, I worked to give positive feelings to the fact that I wouldn't have to do this forever and that my ideal work situation was one where I didn't have to punch a clock or be expected to be at a desk as a part of my job description. By giving out positive feelings to what I wanted, I embarked on a journey governed by the law of attraction that led to me starting The WiseWe Company. Here my commute is short and I'm not required to punch a clock or be at any desk.

How did I arrive in this situation? I got here through unforeseen circumstances, driven simply by love of what I did want, not contempt of what I had. **Remember when I discussed being thankful for our blessings but that we don't have to be satisfied. Well this is what I put into action.**

So, the lesson pertaining to mornings is:

Lesson: Start your day with positive thoughts, not one's of fatigue and negativity

Your thoughts will affect not only the rest of your morning but even the rest of your week. While we can't control what others think, do or say, we can control what we think, do and say so start NOW.

Afternoon and Evening

Happiness comes from the harmony of being alive each second of each minute of everyday and engaging and challenging others to do the same.

The afternoon, evening, really the entire day is governed by a series of habits and communication so pay attention to your habits and communication with yourself and others. Most of us spend our days at work where we are interacting with others. We do have breaks including lunch, so what's the big deal? Well, we spend most of our time at work so it is a big deal.

If you want to make progress, make a profound change and achieve the great goal of changing your reality to match your dreams and vision, then every detail counts. I'm here to tell you that harmony is not a pretty word that was just made up for the fun of it. It means something and in this context, it means that we should work towards a harmony in our life where each element complements the next. So, your job is grueling and you have goals and tough clients. Does that mean you must be tougher and harder or instead a savvy master communicator and navigator of people and interpersonal relationships? Whatever it means that you must be, you shouldn't have to sacrifice your dignity, morals and values.

You should put love first, not money and guess what, the money will come. Love yourself and others enough to tell the truth even in the face of imminent danger. Help others and speak up for others without fear of consequences. A man or woman of faith should only fear God, the divine. By fearing the divine, we are *only* fearful of the divine, which in this case translates into being the best we can be in all situations and always.

During your day, these messages translate into meaningful communications with others.

Lesson: Try and have an interaction and conversation that makes you feel alive.

How do you do that? The first thing you do is approach the interaction with love in your heart. The second thing you do is stick to what you believe but still have respect for the other person or client. Use these guidelines, then sit back and watch the magic happen. What you'll see is more robust interactions where you are engaged NOW, instead of constantly thinking about what you'll do later or in the future.

Lesson: Don't sacrifice the minutes and seconds of NOW, longing for the future.

This is an important lesson because we'll miss out on the journey if we simply get along and get by.

Deposits:

1) Cultivate the habit of not only doing your job but do more than your job entails.
2) Don't always work harder but sometimes smarter is the way to go. You decide.
3) Foster relationships with others so that when you need it, help is there. Also, you learn from people and may be able to help them as well. Karma will reward all positive parties (Negative too..... with negative).
4) Ask questions. Not only does it show interest but the answer might just surprise you. Don't assume because you never know what the other person might be thinking or all the possible parameters surrounding an issue. Don't be afraid to ask and either get an answer or find out that your boss, colleague or client doesn't know. Questions will help you to grow and gain greater insight into things large and small.
5) Don't always need an answer. While it's great to ask questions, don't feel like you always need an answer. If you truly do need one, then the universe will align energy in a proper manner and bring the answer to you.
6) Learn something new every day and recognize when you do. Your daily journey is happening for a reason so it's wise to take note of things large and small. Some have recommended keeping a journal and I wouldn't disagree. I would however keep one from a certain standpoint, an optimistic abundant one. If something happened and you didn't care for it much, capture what you learned from it and in the future what you can do.
7) Always work on your mindset. It's OK to be frustrated or angry but be AWARE that you are. Then you can consciously guide yourself out of that mood and use that energy for productivity and towards an abundant perspective.

Lesson Recap:

- Learn to control your emotions.
- Start your day with positive thoughts, not thoughts of fatigue and negativity.
- Try and have an interaction and conversation that makes you feel alive.
- Don't sacrifice the minutes and seconds of NOW, longing for the future.

WIN AT LIFE – BUILD A BUSINESS. DESTROY FEAR AND DOUBT

As a business owner or someone thinking of starting a new business or running with a new idea, peace of mind is a major goal. You don't want to be forever worrying and having sleepless nights. It's no secret that the road of entrepreneurship and business growth can be rough but some pitfalls and challenges can be avoided. Also, the initial growth phase with all its challenges and pitfalls could be shortened, if some steps are followed. First, you need a plan no matter what you do and how quickly you want to do it.

Let's say you want to have a massive impact on your business and increase efficiencies within the next 6 months. For example, trying to complete a big initiative or project every quarter over the next year to drastically change the trajectory of your company takes a plan and approach. Big goals not only take planning but also strategy and sometimes thinking outside of the norm. This can help you and your business not only keep pace with competitors but drastically change that relationship with them as well. You could compete or just change the dynamic entirely and dominate your space.

Whether you're a teacher, government worker, or business person, how can you be the very best at what you do? How can you both dominate your space while at the same time having piece of mind? Perhaps the answer is by not worrying about who is trying to compete with you but providing so much value to your students, constituents or customers, that anything you're up against is not a barrier at all. With peace of mind comes freedom, happiness and ultimately winning at life. That's what we've explored in this book. I've shared my journey and the lessons and experiences along the way. My goal is to equip you with the necessary tools, inspire and motivate you to fulfill your purpose and achieve your biggest goals. We started in the first half of the book, **Win at Life – The Foundation and Lessons** exploring and building a strong foundation. Now, we'll continue to introduce concepts and lessons that lead to solutions and ultimately winning at life.

WiseWe Mission Statement for Clients

That's our mission statement and mantra for our clients. Our goal is to offer peace of mind so that our clients can sleep at night knowing that there's a partner that has their back with human capital, dedication and a passion to succeed. With our current largest client, we started off contracted for just 10 hours a week of project management work. Now we have a team dedicated towards their success.

Path to Clarity

The Mind is a delicate machine and you should be careful what you feed it (garbage in and garbage out). Put too much garbage in and this leads to the opposite of being clear and focused towards your goals. If you want to remain clear, you need to work on minimizing noise and maximizing your action towards goals.

Clarity is deeply tied to how much distraction you naturally and voluntarily allow as well. Natural distraction can come from a variety of sources such as the general sounds and conversations in life, commercials, advertisements (billboards, magazine ads, etc.), news and much more. Minimize your intake of these various sources of noise and distraction; instead, give that time to meditation, prayer and action.

Many of these distractions are involuntary and you may not be directly seeking these information sources but they are right in your face with information that isn't necessarily keeping you on task regarding your vision and goals. Before you get into any advanced planning or organizational techniques at a fundamental level, you must:

- Organize around your mindset/way or seeing or dealing with things/perspective
- Beliefs/Mindset fuels strategy that drives business and personal plan of goal attainment/action

In the first half of the book, **Win at Life – The Foundation and Lessons**, I talk about a positive mindset and how I was able to build one. A positive growth mindset can lead to your successes and growth both personally and in business. Seek out what that means and you'll start off with a great foundation.

Strategically Win

A good strategy can float the ship, win the game, and win the war. A bad strategy or just the wrong strategy could lose them all for you too. Strategy determines the overarching guidance you'll use to get from point A to B. It is the factor that will affect your decisions, goals, and action steps.

As I discuss in **Win at Life – The Foundation and Lessons**, prior to moving to Miami, I didn't necessarily have a strategy. In a world with unlimited possibilities and paths to take, a strategy can point you in one direction or the other. Give some serious thought and analysis to your career, personal and business strategies because they will help you make daily decisions and do the daily work necessary to achieve your goals.

After Miami, I set the sail. I would gain clients by simply seeking valuable life/work experiences, doing a good job and building my network. My strategy was not to have a big marketing budget and explain why I'm the best entrepreneur or consultant. I knew I would have to be known and known for doing a good job to have staying power. That was my strategy, to have a slow methodical approach where eventually, I wouldn't have to look for work but work and people would seek me out for my knowledge, experience and unique platform.

This strategy matched the industry that I was entering quite well and one opportunity led to the next opportunity until I now have a good network and reputation. The strategy influenced the decisions that I made, including the projects I would work on or people I would do business with. Additionally, ethics and values are a centerpiece and determining factor of projects I take on. You might be saying, well Wayne of course naturally. Not that I doubt you but we're talking about the Business Management Consulting industry where Billions of dollars are at play every day in projects from building submarines to software that run banks.

Ethics and Values weren't necessarily things I was seeing requested in high profile projects or businesses. This is what I wanted to stand for and decided I would look for clients who shared the same universal ideals of positively impacting our community and the world. This is how I would set out to be successful and make profits doing what I loved and stood for.

I knew that people, process and technology was central to my industry and really business so I began focusing on these three elements, building expertise in all 3 areas. I was naturally analytical and had a goal to grow this skill to be able to analyze any business and business situation to give the necessary feedback or advice. I became a business process design and redesign expert. To a large degree, to successfully run your business and your personal life with all the goals and action items to match, you need to be able to analyze and re-analyze as new information comes in or things change. This is an invaluable skill and necessary iterative step to take throughout your journey.

Design of a Lifetime

Before you apply technology as a solution to a personal or business problem, start with the people and process involved. Let's take the solution of a cellphone. Or better yet, let's take the solution of a smartphone, a web enabled device that allows you to surf on the web, watch videos, download and listen to music. All great, right?! While it is great to relax and have fun, if you give the cellphone to someone with a growth mindset and a clear strategy and life plan, they can use that smart device as a solution to assist them in achieving goals.

Give that same smart device to someone with a fixed mindset, who only is interested in the phone for its entertainment value, then you will get a different result. You might have someone who uses the phone primarily to listen to music, watch videos and talk trash with their buddies or girlfriends. This is by the way totally natural and stuff we all do but the idea is to minimize those activities that don't bear positive results and maximize those activities on the phone that do.

This is not to pass judgment on anyone but rather to point out how the same individual can use technology in two different ways. For example, does your to-do-list include calls or emails that need to be made. Are you in the creative business and need to create a video for your organization? Well, one way to increase your output is to do less of the non-producing activities and more of the producing activities that are tied to your vision, strategy, goals, etc.

We are all given the same amount of time in a day. Instead of thinking or even saying to yourself that the next man or woman must have more time than me or less to worry about, why not look at yourself and see if everything that you and/or your organization is doing is the most efficient and effective.

A cellphone is one example that everyone can relate to. Taking the technology aspect further, let's say that we're talking about a COTS (commercial off the shelf) or SAAS (software as a service) cloud based technology. These are technologies that municipalities like cities and states, corporations and businesses of all shapes and sizes may use. The point is the same. In these cases, the stakeholders or executives who want to see this new technology implemented must not overlook the people or end users of the system. Stakeholders should make sure that the input of the end users of the system is included in the implementation or building of the new system. It's just as important to communicate that this technology will not fix or replace broken processes, instead people must consciously fix or replace broken processes. The technology itself will only facilitate the task that needs to be achieved.

Organization System

When looking at your organization system, the suggestion is simple. No, literally it is to keep it simple whether in your individual or business life. Normally and first you must take what is currently complex and break it down into simpler terms and a simpler form/structure hierarchy. Not only for an entrepreneur but also for a middle manager, CEO, just about everyone, there are some basic categories that you should have an electronic and paper filing system for. Breaking it down to the following categories can be a suggested end goal to replicate on the computer, USB, file cabinet and file folder:

Daily Agenda

Your Daily Agenda should consist of the plans that you have created for your family, yourself and business or career:

- Daily Agenda
  - Personal Development Plan
  - Family Plan
  - Business Plan
  - Career Plan
  - Clear Bills and Debt

You can add just a business OR career plan if you wish to only focus on being an entrepreneur for life. It also doesn't hurt to leverage your options and have a plan b (career) but if you're 1000% committed, then you can just have the one folder. I'd also add clear bills and debt because we shouldn't ignore that the society we live in and if you're like me and everyone I know, then financial freedom is right at the top of your list, to do list, etc. So, we list it here to be on your daily radar along with your plans. Within each of those main folders, you may have what you think you'll need. We work with our clients at a greater level of detail, creating subfolders as well. Of course, first we learn much more about them and work together on goals, before getting to a finer level of detail.

In addition to your Daily Agenda, you will then have a more archival list of items that you work on longer term. While not necessarily every day, these items are just as important as you may visit and update these files every other day. You should have a file for every household member. So for a wife and husband with a boy and a girl, it should look like this. I try and keep files to 5 for simplicity so we'll combine everyone into a large family file with sub folders:

Weekly Files
- Family
  o Husband (actual name) not husband)
  o Wife
  o Son
  o Daughter
- Home
- Insurance
- Taxes
- Finances
  o Bank
  o Credit
- Business **BONUS**

You can then add more subfolders as needed and pertinent to your specific situation. Once again as life coaches and Business Management Consultants, we work with select individuals and corporations on structuring these in great detail.

Filing

Once you get organized with your categories, I truly believe that it is best to use the KISS Principal (Keep it Simple Stupid). No, you are not stupid but this principal is essentially pointing towards translating process into the simplest terms possible, not only for duplication but explanation if necessary.

The following filing system is recommended for a basic setup:

- 2 Drawer filing cabinet
    - o Two rows of hanging files for each heads of household (husband and wife)
    - o Folders represent categories above
- Portfolio
    - o Slots represent categories above
    - o This is day to day file system
    - o You may need or update the types of documents contained in your portfolio daily

Shredding

- Purchase a shredder if within your means to do so and shred at least once a week
- Research and populate calendar with FREE shredding events in your area.

Trash/Recycle

Obviously, you can't recycle away everything, like food, etc. Whatever you can recycle, do so because it only aides in improving the planet and our environment, cutting down on waste and being more efficient. If we all do our part, then we can have a positive impact.

From an organization standpoint, you don't need a bunch of items in your space that you aren't using and just crowd you unnecessarily. Get in the habit of NOT hoarding or stockpiling but recycling what you can and throwing away what you must. Many organizations, especially large companies, already have standardized recycling and trash pickup and disposal including policies and procedures for cycling out old equipment and furniture. If you're a smaller company or one that doesn't have as robust a trash/recycling program as you could, it only helps to re-evaluate and create any needed changes for efficiency. The same goes if you are an individual. Some municipalities only pick up recycling and trash on certain days and not often enough. Also, they may not pick up everything that you need to dispose of. You should create a general trash/recycling plan that works for you. Many municipalities have a dump that you can drive to for trash and recycling. There are also options for giving items away.

Donations

Do you have a storage unit with items that you've been saving for years? Or perhaps you're just storing items in your basement, garage or other storage area. Maybe there are old baby toys and clothes or papers from middle school, high school or college. Why not keep a few treasured items but donate the baby clothes and toys.

When you're truly going from *Clutter to Clarity*, it should be a multi-faceted approach covering every part of your life. This is the best way to get the most impact and effective change that you're seeking. Your environment or the space you keep and maintain goes into the "chi" or spirit of the space. An organized and inspirational space is more likely to motivate then a cluttered space overflowing with unneeded or worse, unwanted items.

While writing this book, I undertook the process of going through a storage unit that our family had for less than a year. After I moved my wife (at the time) and kid back from Florida to Maryland, we rented a storage unit. After a few months though, I wanted to see if this was truly needed. There were several benefits to closing the unit, including not only cost savings but importantly the ability to GIVE to those who needed what we could offer. There were some unopened toys and clothes in great shape. While we held on to a few memento clothing items, we mostly donated the rest. Perfect time too (December)!

Clutter to Clarity

To achieve peace of mind in business, you first need to address some fundamentals before you can really take your business, big idea or initiative to the next level. This will allow you the ability to grow and not be tripped up by simple challenges, where mechanisms could be put in place from the beginning or even midstream as a fix. It's better to fix something that's broken and prepare for growth then not to fix at all.

ORGANIZE FOR SUCCESS AND PROFITS

Revisit Business Plan

At any stage, it's important to revisit your business plan, including your marketing, operations and financial plans. It's not only good for the CEO to know these metrics but of course in many instances specialists and staff in general should as well. What is your mission statement? This is probably something that's not going to change when revisiting your business plan. However, what might change is the marketing strategy which includes the ways you're planning to go after your target market. In fact, your customer data might even show that your target market should be different than what it currently is.

Things are harder to share if they're all word-of-mouth and contained in conversations at meetings. You not only need meeting minutes that can be shared but you also need a general document that your executives can reference and point to when leading teams, building a strategy for teams, and implementing the overall business plan.

Additionally, sometimes the industry or competitors can cause you to reanalyze your business plan to make sure that you remain competitive and one step ahead. Imagine creating a business plan and then 10 or 20 years into the growth of the company you have never revisited the plan to update. That wouldn't make sense and many businesses are pretty good at updating a marketing strategy or analyzing financial statements and readjusting some things. However, companies are less likely to revisit the business plan comprehensively and do an analysis of all the various parts.

Business Plan Summary of Main Components:

1. Mission Statement
2. Marketing Plan
3. Financial Plan
4. Operating Plan
5. Human Resources Plan
6. Legal Structure and Plan

I've started 3 iterations of a consulting company, having different business plans for each one. My very first consulting company was for musicians helping specifically with management and marketing. This target market has its own unique characteristics, so of course we couldn't service the same way we would a government entity seeking a software implementation partner. The plan here centered around connecting with musicians and having a unique plan for each one. With the second company we received some good and free help from PTAP, a division of the SBA. Our basic plan was to establish ourselves as a traditional consulting company with the ability to work on government as well as private contracts. PTAP helped us to create an even more detailed plan with especially important action steps and milestones to become a legitimate consulting company.

During this process, we learned a lot about the industry because this free accountability partner urged us to research and put the proper pieces in place. We still did our music events to connect with the community. All our efforts led to a job offer from a larger company where I could learn more about the consulting industry, project management and business analysis. The business plan of the WiseWe Company has been a combination of the 2 previous plans combining community, value and profitability. It's been the best of all worlds. Our target market focus, at least initially, adjusted from government to the private sector. Also, financially, we have a model that allows us to self-finance the whole business.

What are we planning on doing next with all this knowledge and years of experience? One thing that we want to do is teach all who are interested how to be a consultant in your preferred area. We'll have a couple of options where I'll help train the next generation of entrepreneurs, consultants, project managers and business analysts. We always advise to seek out the free services available through the SBA and their partners first. Once you've gone through that experience then you could seek out additional help.

Marketing

Marketing and sales really go hand in hand. If you're going to attain clients then you need them to be aware of your product or service. That's the marketing part which will involve those methods by which you inform people what your company has to offer. Methods could include print, audio, video or other means. Sales should be tightly connected to marketing because what if someone comes knocking and is interested. That's when selling takes over from marketing and you'll need a process to close deals. I draw on a few important lessons from retail sales.

First, does your customer have a genuine interest in what you're selling. It's like when someone walks into a store out of interest. Don't be afraid to do some market testing and see whether people actually want your product. After that, put some thought and planning into the package and presentation. How many times have you walked into a store with very low prices but everything was out of order and you couldn't find anything you were interested in. What did you do? Probably walk right back out.

Along with presentation, quality is of the utmost importance as well. Once the customer engages with your product, is there a high quality that holds and peaks their interest even more. While the customer is engaging with your product, it's your job to be guiding them through the process by asking the right questions to gauge their deeper level of need. Through the process of asking questions, you may encounter objections or issues that the customer presents. That's a natural part of the process and instead of getting turned off or flustered, expect it and even practice how to overcome common objections. In my opinion, the best way to overcome objections is to truly understand them so you can effectively address the customer and maybe even improve your product or process as well. However, what you should try not to change is your pricing unless it's extremely low. There's no winning the game of low price or better yet it's probably one you don't want to win.

Sales

Sales are important to any business so I don't need to tell you to focus on sales or converting prospects into customers. All I'll say here is once again your end to end solution can also help you manage this. Let's look at two of the most popular tools out there for lead generation. One is (once again you guessed it) Salesforce and the other is LinkedIn Sales Navigator. Specifically, within Salesforce there is data.com. There are also other tools out there for lead generation as well. Whatever you use, you'll want the ability to filter with specific criteria that matches your target market. Now what I'm describing obviously is for more of a B to B situation than a B to C. For B to C, you may want to focus more on ads including social media ads on Facebook, YouTube and/or Google. Social Media Management including ad management is a new area of service offering for us; however, the good news is that the social media platforms make it pretty straightforward to create and run your ads. This process will really be a three-point process of confirming your target market that's number one. Number two will be the creation and design of your ad campaign. Number three is to assess budget or how much to spend on your ad campaign. A high-quality ad with a well-committed budget can positively affect your desired outcome of reaching more of the market and converting them into customers.

Whether B to B or B to C, sales at its core is largely the same. There is the presentation and perception of your business and service or product offering. There is preparation and actions that you take to craft that presentation and perception so that the marketplace places a value on your business that you desire. Then there's the sales process that may start with that presentation, awareness, perception and then end in a lifetime committed customer. Continue to focus on that entire process for success and make sure to invest in the proper tools to support it.

When organizing for the financial success of your business, <u>plan and track as much as possible.</u> Also, how will you fund your business? Will you accept investments or bootstrap with your own money? Zero in on and do the following:

1. <u>Determine Financing Strategy:</u>
The type of business you have could very well determine whether you're seeking investment or not. There are other factors that can determine this as well so create your business plan and seek good, free advice in the beginning from some of the resources that I've shared like SCORE. You will need to determine whether you will:

   a. Bootstrap?
   b. Seek Investors?
   c. Seek Loans?
   d. Mix of all OR other type

To bootstrap means that YOU will provide the funding your business needs to operate and grow. This will come either from working a job and/or your savings. Bootstrapping is a legitimate method of startup financing so if you're only considering investments or loans to start your business, think again. For example, if you're starting a dog-walking business and think you'll need a loan or investor, STOP and seek some free expert advice first. A high tech, software or bio science company might need to take on investment and loans for R&D and highly skilled labor. An entrepreneur starting an accounting practice might not. Why? Because the costs to start are lower and the accountant might just need his laptop and business cards to get started, using the money he makes to re-invest in the business.

2. Accountant/QuickBooks

Accountants have been trained in the discipline of keeping the books, so let them do their job and keep yours. At the very least, keep your own books and provide your accountant what they need during tax time. As mentioned already, use your own accounting software as well for banking and invoices. QuickBooks is a popular software that can be linked to your banking software. This all makes it easier when it's time to share information with the IRS or your Accountant.

Track everything coming in and going out – expenses and income

There are some simple, low cost tools for doing this. Many banks offer software that will allow you to categorize your expenses. If you're able to add notes to these expenses, then that may be the only tool you'll need. More than likely, you'll need to use your bank software in tandem with another tool. Those items will be your foundation for tracking expenses and income. Add on top of that a popular accounting software like QuickBooks to pay people and collect payment. QuickBooks also can sync with your bank account, so then you'll have the ability to pay people, collect payment, track and categorize expenses and add notes for any other important details related to the daily expense incurred. These notes should be anything that can assist when completing your quarterly and annual taxes.

QuickBooks

Whether starting your business, growing your business or for established businesses, you always want to have your hand on the pulse of financials. QuickBooks has always been one of the leaders in this space allowing you to manage your finances by connecting with your bank account and reconciling. QuickBooks also allows you to manage your invoices by creating, sending and closing invoices sent to customers as well. Because a business uses QuickBooks to manage these financial components, it's also a benefit during tax season. Even before tax season, you can invite your CPA into your QuickBooks experience so that they have access to the information they will need to manage your taxes. You want to make sure to have a QuickBooks manager on staff or someone trained on how to manage your QuickBooks. This is another service The WiseWe Company offers that includes reconciliation, group/individual training for your office professionals. Additionally, for startups growing businesses and even established businesses, if you need it, there are apps that you can connect with QuickBooks such as Fundbox in the event you're seeking financing in the form of invoice factoring. No matter what tool you use, you will need software to manage your expenses, income, invoices, and financial statements. This is what you receive with QuickBooks and why it has been an industry leader and critical tool for businesses of all sizes.

3. Know Your Numbers

There are key numbers of your business that you should know and be aware of. One reason is that investors will ask for this information. If you're not seeking investment money, knowing your key numbers will help you to make decisions and measure your business performance. Business costs to be aware of include:

    a. Cost of Customer Acquisition
    b. Product or Service Cost
    c. The Rate you should be paid based on the market and your experience and/or product
    d. Be familiar and comfortable with statements:
        i. Income Statement
        ii. Balance Sheet
        iii. Cash Flow

Operations

Operations covers how your business functions daily and in what areas. It's important to write everything down. This will help you to fully understand how things are working and identify any weak areas, risks, bottlenecks, etc. There should be a process for everything and writing it down will force you to clearly define the process and ensure owners, employees, clients and end users are on the same page. You will grow your business by having systems in place that allow you to insert additional employees and clients into the systems.

Systemize Everything!!

Why? Your primary objective besides turning a profit is replacing yourself. Check out the E-Myth book which does a wonderful job at covering the difference between a true entrepreneur and someone who just creates a job for themselves – manager vs. entrepreneur.

Areas to systemize include:
- Business Operations
- Business Development
- Marketing
- Sales
- Accounting
- New Product Development

If you can think of an area of your business, chances are you should systemize it. Not only do the work but map the work. Map how you do everything so you can train someone else to do it. This is also a form of engineering a process and can further help if you need to re-engineer for a more efficient process. Other reasons for system:

- So that potential investors know you have one
- See if any competitive edge can be gained through your processes

Understand that your business and personal life are connected. The purpose of starting a business will be to make consistent profit and grow. Just because you start a business doesn't mean your personal expenses go away. You'll most likely take a salary and this money will pay your household bills. How much money you're able to contribute to your bills directly affects your kids, wife, parents, siblings, etc.

Team- CPA, Attorney, Payroll, Partners

You'll wear many hats starting and growing a business. However, to scale effectively and efficiently, you'll need to assemble a team to handle a few crucial aspects of your business. Sure, you could do your own taxes but there's much more to hiring a CPA than doing your taxes. A good CPA will first consult with you to understand your needs and help you with your tax strategy first. There's a host of services that a CPA offers to keep your business on track when it comes to tax compliance. In addition to doing your annual taxes, there are annual forms to file as well. If you use contractors, they'll help you prepare and distribute your 1099s. Your tax strategy could lead them to setting up or administering other items as well, even helping to determine a salary that you'll pay yourself. A payroll company will ensure that this salary is distributed appropriately to you with all of the necessary state and federal taxes being withdrawn and paid throughout the year. Or you may decide to hold those funds in escrow and pay at the end of the year. What they do as part of that initial consultation is to determine your payroll strategy - yes there's strategy to everything. In addition to yourself, your employees will also be on payroll and the payroll company will help keep you compliant with taxes including unemployment insurance. Employees will help you run the company providing the necessary internal and external services needed to meet the demands of customers and the company.

We realize that the consultative process that a company goes through starting a business (score, consultants, etc.) and managing taxes (cpa) also extends to recruiting and hiring. That's why the WiseWe Company offers consultative services in this area and even can take it a step further by providing the team. In some instances, we provide team members for fast growing companies who prefer not to embark on a recruiting campaign. Since we've already learned the company as analysts and consultants, making recommendations for tools, strategy, etc., we're well positioned and equipped to provide further assistance. Some of this assistance includes Salesforce help desk implementation /management or implementation support (project management). In this regard, we're a strategic human resource partner.

Questions:

1. Have you assembled your team? Where are you weak?
2. Happy and clear on your tax strategy?
3. Do you have your operational tools in place? What do you use to manage finance, accounting, operations, customer service and project management? What are the tools used for each? Is there also a mapped-out process to accompany the tool?

Right People

First, **understand that your business and personal life are connected**. Right people = Team, both business and personal that can support your vast undertaking, emotionally, physically, etc.

Structure your life to be positive = Your clients will be seeking solutions. If your life approach is negative, how will you bring people together to solve challenges and inspire your existing and new clients?

Family

Your family must be financially prepared for your journey. You need to plan personal expenses and how they will be paid month to month. If you bootstrap and borrow money from family and friends, you will need to clearly outline a payback structure or stock options.

Mentors

A good mentor will help enlighten you along your path to success and profits, offering good advice through experience and recommendations (tools, connections, etc.). Advice and recommendations can save you money because it's coming from those in your desired industry who have already gone through what you are going through.

Positive Life

Execution – Change Management. Design the start, beginning and end with some energizing, motivating, and inspiring routines. Change will happen early and often and this is a methodology to help.
Examples:
- Prayer
- Meditation
- Reflection on what you're thankful for
- Envisioning successfully completing or attaining goals
- EXERCISE
- Positive reinforcement through sayings….

The idea is to create your own empowering routine that gets you in the right frame of mind with the proper energy level as well.

Body

Execution – Ability to physically and mentally last for 8-24 hours of work a day. If you're in the consulting business, billable hours worked = $, which leads to profits. The better you perform, the sharper you are, the more you can do for a client, the more work you may get = more billable hours = More $= More profits.

Treat your body like it's precious = When business takes off or is even struggling and needs to take off, you will need to be strong to work the long hours or take road trips. Improve and challenge yourself to be better always

= Starts with you and translates for your clients and colleagues.

Be Better

Challenge yourself to be better and you will not only add personal value but continue to add value for your clients. Each new skill you learn or knowledge you acquire can have a positive impact on discovering something new for clients or offering more value to them as well. Maybe if you're providing one service or product, focusing on constant growth and improvement can lead to providing other services or products.

UTILIZE PROJECT MANAGEMENT – IT'S NOT JUST FOR PMPS

Project Management is something to be addressed by all growing companies because project management is not just a buzzword or something that PMPs do. You should utilize project management tools, techniques and strategies within your business. That way you have a structure to turn cases and suggestions into trackable issues, risks, and short and long-term projects.

For project management, there are a couple of resources that you can refer to. There is the Project Management Institute (PMI) and the PMBOK Guide. Through that organization and in that book, you can learn a lot about the discipline of project management. I've had the privilege of receiving on the job training for project management before I even read the PMBOK Guide for the first time. If you take PMI classes or read the guide, apply the information learned to truly develop your skills and add value to your organization.

At the heart of project management is the purpose of managing variables for an outcome. The main variables include the project milestones, tasks, the people committed to completing the task, the time duration of the tasks, that all comprise a schedule with dates. Also included would be tracking issues, risks and controlling budget. But project management, of course, is much more than that and can't be summarized within this book.

The guide mentioned above is really the industry reference for this discipline. What you learn most through the study and application of project management is that there is not one way to administer project management for every single project. A good project manager knows that each project requires a unique project plan. This doesn't mean that you can't have a standard template or series of steps. What it does mean is that each time you initiate a project, you still must account for any unique variables. For our clients, we have of course used Microsoft Project.

Recently, through implementing Salesforce, we rely more so on Salesforce apps. There are also other tools that you can use for project management so you want to understand your business and the types of projects you are managing. Then, you'll want to do an analysis of the tools in the marketplace so that you can arrive at a good fit for your business. Next, you'll want to administer and use the tools for project management. That will involve change management so the team can adapt and start using the tools on a daily basis. Even if you have a dedicated project manager, project management is a contact team sport.

Project Management Elements
1. Task
2. Person(s) to Complete Task
3. Budget
4. Milestones
5. Deliverable Dates
6. More Project Management

Reference Links
1. Project Management Institute
2. PMBOK Guide
3. Microsoft Project
4. Asana
5. Trello
6. Basecamp

Apply Project Management

Apply discipline of Project Management to achieve constant growth, improvement, skills and knowledge. Project management processes fall into five groups:
- Initiating
- Planning
- Executing
- Monitoring and Controlling
- Closing

We've already covered 4 of these areas in our own way. The journal that we discussed earlier can be broken down into a few categories. Capture and measure to design, plan and control improvement:

- Body (Exercise Regimen and Diet
- Family
- Business
- Children as separate and special category
- Positivity – Capture daily lessons or reinforcements from e-mentors and others

Calendar

Schedule - THE MOST IMPORTANT THING is to execute the items on your calendar. It's not good enough to schedule them in but you must DO them as well. Who completes EVERYTHING on their calendar ALL of the time?? There needs to be a sense of urgency in completing these items. Start by doing the things that will have the greatest IMPACT or as Brian Tracy likes to say CONSEQUENCES on your business life. Do as many of these throughout your day as possible. You should fill your day with creating VALUE for customers or yourself/business OR making SALES. Why? Because ultimately your business livelihood is about making money through delivering tremendous value.

Project Management Perspective- Review and Summary

Project Management knowledge draws on ten areas:

Integration
Blend areas of your business and or personal life together using lessons, knowledge and topics discussed

Cost
Conduct cost benefit analyses with family, colleagues, etc. Track businesses and personal expenses – keep separate)

Human Resources
Organize for Profits – Hire the right people. Be slow to hire, then focus on replacing yourself.

Stakeholder Management

There are many parties involved in your business journey. Determine how everyone fits into the puzzle. Manage and foster relationships.

Scope

What fits into your plan? Scope of Work – Defined summary of project – what it's generally about and general expectations.

Quality

Make sure what you are providing is done to the best of your ability. Give 110% effort. QC yourself with periodic evaluations and checks. Have other people conduct QC check.

Risk Management

Track and Monitor major barriers or bottlenecks

Have a plan / strategy for all 3 and manage with tools:

- Communications
- Time
- Procurement

Tools

Other tools besides a journal and the financial tools we have mentioned can help you Project Manage 10 Areas (Monitor and Control). Software tools should help you organize, manage and communicate in a few areas:

- Tasks
- Contacts
- Organizations
- Opportunities
- Projects – About, History, Emails Notes, Files, Milestones, Tasks, and Events
- Emails
- Reports
- Project Based
- Discussion
- To-Do List
- File
- Text Document
- Event
- Email Content to Project
- Invite People to Participate

Rituals/Habits/Routines (Closing)

Habits - A good habit to develop is a SENSE OF URGENCY. I could teach you about calendar alerts of various kinds but instead, I want you to write down this goal of having a sense of urgency about your To Do List or Calendar. Nothing that anyone can tell or teach you can replace the need for you to WHAT? **GET IT DONE!**

Decisions (Closing)

Decisions affect whether:

- You're happy or not
- Have the energy necessary to work the long hours starting a business
- Have the support you need
- Whether you procrastinate or not
- Start the right business
- Grow the business in the most profitable way

Research and advice may tell you to act in one way but ultimately the direction your business takes is up to you. Decide to do these things:

- Exercise
- Knowledge
- Library
- Books and Audiobooks
- Higher Education
- Groups
- Mentors
- References and Resources

Can't Get Hired? – Create Your Experience and Job!

When you do start that great company, there will be some key components that can't be overlooked including great customer service.

EXCEL AT CUSTOMER SERVICE

Many people work in a customer service position of some sort. For kids starting off in the workplace, there are some basic principles of customer service. This is how I learned customer service and sales and while many call it an old school approach, to me it just seems like the right approach. You can tell when a cashier, waitress, telephone representative, banker or mechanic, etc. embodies the principles I'll describe. You can certainly tell when they do not as well.

Why Talk about Customer Service?

Customer Service transcends industry and is really about standards. What standards have you set for yourself and your life? This impacts what level of service you will expect to receive and give in life. If service isn't that important to you, then maybe you'll shop at a store with unfriendly, transactional workers and broken processes. If service is important to you, then maybe you'll shop at a more discerning store where the workers are friendlier and the process is seamless.

Does it really matter? Well, you have a choice and to me it matters. It's like the saying "it's not what people call you, but what you answer to". Will you just accept any kind of communication and shop at any kind of store? Or do you want to shop where the value is greatest, not only in the products but the organization too.

First, let's talk about some communication fundamentals that will help to illuminate the topic of customer service and then take us into a discussion of the relationship that exists between you, your business and your customers. This represents the output of your designed life where you've created the experience and now reap what you've sown.

Communication Matters

As many of you know, not only verbal, but non-verbal communication matters as well. You can say just as much with your eyes and body language as you can with your words. In my college textbook, 'Introducing Communication Theory, Analysis and Appreciation', authors West and Turner defined it as "a process in which individuals employ symbols to establish and interpret meaning in their environment" (West / Turner, 4). It's important to study and pay attention to these symbols so that you can master the key to effective communication.

You ultimately want your message to get across, correct? If your message is to convince someone why they should buy your product or service, then you'll need to be as effective as possible. One process that I think can show effective communication or horrible communication easily is retail sales. I started my work career, more or less, in retail. I learned the basic components of client interaction from a fundamental level, yet that level was so high, it is still rare that I see it today.

Let's look at customer service communication through the lens of my retail work experience that I believe was fundamental, classic and effective customer service and communication.

Smile

First, when someone enters your work area or store, etc., you should greet them with a smile. Greet them with a smile not because you want to be phony and pretend you're happy, but because you ARE happy!! Now if you're in retail sales and NOT happy then we should take a step back and discuss why you have more reasons to be happy then not.

If you can master the fundamental lessons and structure that retail sales has to offer then, you can do very well within that job. You can also take those same skills and climb within the company to a higher or different position. These skills also are applicable to other industries and positions as well. Customer Service is the foundation for many industries and businesses. When you smile, you're acknowledging that you're happy with what you're doing and happy to see the customer or client that is helping to pay your salary. Get happy and stay happy knowing these things or find another job.

I enjoyed the challenge of retail, including its incomparable components:

- Display and presentation of product
- Verbal communication of product
- Non-verbal communication of product
- Selling the benefit of various products
- Matching the right product with the customer
- Overcoming objections
- Knowing when to stop pushing and save for another day

Display and Presentation of Product

If your product is on the floor when a customer comes into your store and people are walking on it, then do you think it's an appealing buy? Maybe some places, but not most I would suspect. A better idea and practice is to present your merchandise or service in the best light possible. For another business besides retail, that might mean having a website that lays out your product offerings simply and elegantly. The simple part will help customers immediately understand what you are offering. The elegant part will evoke positive emotion that can lead to a purchase or investment.

Clothing should be labelled with a price tag and the inner tag should describe what materials the artifact is made of. That is essentially what the customer needs to know in addition to any current sales specials. You would want the same basic layout for a website of services, to include the service, what that service is comprised of OR another way to say it is what the customer will be paying for. When a potential customer envisions themselves using the service, what do they see?

Pricing is a little less straightforward within service sales and you should consult a professional to help you determine if you will list your prices on your website or not.

Verbal Communication of Product

Once the product presentation and your warm smile welcome a customer into your store or business website, then there should be a conversion process in place. This will usually start with a greeting such as welcome to [store name], can I help you find anything today? If no, then offer your name and let the customer know you can be of assistance if they need. Stay close enough to the customer to help if needed but not so close that they feel crowded or like they're being followed. If the customer wants to see any of your product, show them and explain features and pricing when needed.

Use this interactive opportunity to discover what in general your customer is trying to achieve? This will help you offer other products that you may have as well. This provides a greater benefit to customers who will get more than they initially came for.

Wherever I go, I seem to notice either excellent customer service or the breakdown in customer service due to either a broken process or the company/employee be unware of any other way. As a consultant, this doesn't even come close to the detailed analysis and solutions that we have the capability to provide. However, I don't believe in holding information back especially if you have the expertise and insight to shed light on something for another boss.

I've worked for some great companies and I remember working for one industry leader in their discount department. The store is probably the number one department store and has amazing departments which include a discount department which has now branched into their own separate stores. This was truly a store that believed in treating both customers and each other with respect. They still believed in the customer was always right philosophy but at least at the location where I worked, the manager always asked for respect all around. I can remember a time when someone from another department came to our department and made a disparaging comment about our discount department. The store manager got wind of this comment and very soon the employee was fired. The manager believed that no one employee or department was so special where disrespect was an ok thing.

HR Matters – A Great Partner Can Go A long Way

At The WiseWe Company, we have supported one of our client's growth of 80+ new clients in 2 years by providing a one-stop shop for many services and ultimate peace of mind. As part of our managed services we have established and managed:

- **Client Services** – providing management and team to support 700+ end user organizations of software
- **Project Management** – disciplined approach and organization to nearly 100+ implementations over 3 years
- **Repositories** – implemented and managed confidential files in 3 different well-known repository solutions
  - o **SharePoint**
  - o **DropBox**
  - o **Box**
- **Salesforce** – manage setup and implementation of end to end solution
- **New Website Build by Vendor** - oversee and worked with website vendor to meet specifications of client for new website.
- **Software Training** – learned software of our client – currently create and update user guides and training videos.

In addition to the software training we conduct for the 700+ end users, we also offer **QuickBooks Training** and support. We start by understanding our clients' specific needs and then customize the solution for their requirements. A recommendation from our client follows:

A managed services company could be a great partner for many reasons. A few are:

1.Hiring can be complex and expensive with no guarantees.
   a. **The right partner can be a one stop shop for your operational hiring needs**
2.It's hard to run the business and be the one changing it at the same time.
   a. **The right partner can offer a fresh perspective to take your wishes and fulfill them in a cutting edge, effective and efficient way without disrupting operations**

Client Services

Imagine that you have a partner who can run your customer service operations and scale up on demand as you grow. No hassle with recruiting and hiring, just quality staff on demand and at your disposal. One way that we ensure that this is possible is build out capacity on our staff pipeline of team members with the same basic customer service training. This training by the way isn't so basic anymore and was highlighted in our earlier section on customer service.

There's a way that customer service used to be done and the way that the best companies do it today. We have team members who were formally trained from some of those best companies and then we add the additional layer of WiseWe customer service training.

Journey to Win at Life

When I hear people using the term self-made, I cringe because no one is really self-made. Along our journeys, many people either directly or indirectly help, influence, inspire, motivate or do the opposite. Even those who detract, doubt, gossip, hate on or just plain don't like or support us, help make us who we are. We can take the negativity and turn it into positive action, overcome the naysayers and surpass all expectations. That would be considered indirect influence that helps make the successful who we are.

I remember having a job and someone asking me what I wanted to do or be in life during a casual conversation. When I told them, I planned to be the CEO of my own company, I'll never forget the roar of laughter that erupted. That person helped to make me who I am today, CEO of The WiseWe Company. I'm not self-made. Instead I'm a product of doubters AND supporters. I'm a product of the journey that included wins and losses that all helped me to ultimately Win at Life.

STRATEGIC PARTNER

Organization and re-organization at any stage is important especially for growing companies. Maybe you started off as an LLC when it was just you and/or your cofounder but as you grow perhaps stocks and options are something to consider. If you're a nonstock INC or LLC then expanding through stock ownership will require that you upgrade your business structure. This is only one of the ways to reorganize, you could also open up additional LLCs and move them all under your existing INC structure. Of course, don't do it just to do it but make sure there's good business reason. This is a good opportunity to consult with your team of attorneys and consultants to make sure that as you grow you have the best structure in place to support that growth.

Another way to reorganize is to look at your current tools and processes to determine whether you'll stick with the same or if there's a need for a change. Much of what we've discussed so far in this book pertains to just that, assessing those crucial tools and processes supporting company growth. We can talk about some of our favorites but at the end of the day you'll still want to do a full assessment to determine what's best for your company. There isn't one solution that fits all.

WISEWE TIP:

Don't wait until you reach a critical point to invest in systems, infrastructure and processes for growth. Get ahead of the business growth by investigating and investing now.

Some questions to answer. If you want to connect with us for support, send us the answers to some preliminary questions so we can have a good understanding of where you are now. Answer these for your company:

1. What industry are you in and who are some of your main competitors?
2. What volume of emails do you currently experience?
3. What volume of calls do you currently experience per day?
4. Do you expect that volume to change or remain the same?
5. Is there a good business case for designing for the reception of more calls than emails? Meaning do you want to intentionally guide customers to call instead of email?
6. What functions of a CRM as described do you think you'll most likely need?

Manage Growth

You and your business have big goals and will need a strategy, team, infrastructure, tools and more to achieve them. This is true for businesses of all sizes and at all phases of growth. The details and specifics may be different but what remains the same is the need for a game plan to achieve your goal. I've been on this entrepreneurship journey for 12 years, gained a lot of experience and knowledge about starting and growing projects and businesses. I've learned just as much from listening, watching and interacting with other successful people as well.

A great game plan starts with reflection on what exactly it is that you want to achieve, which will lead to clarity in action. Now simple reflection is rarely enough, which is why we have informal and formal advisors and resources. Resources can include people who have traveled a similar path before and wrote about it like I'm doing in this book. Resources can also include thorough research on the topics or sub-topics that comprise the big goals and milestones you wish to achieve for yourself and/or business.

When I started my first business, I was just testing the waters, seeing if entrepreneurship was within reach. When I started my second business, I was an MBA student and wanted to see capitalism and all that I was studying in action. When I started the WiseWe Company, it was a beautiful combination of WHY + Passion + Persistence + Love + Expertise + Skill + People. Whatever GREAT thing we start will have many elements to it and each should be appreciated, nurtured and grown.

Having worked in customer service and operational environments for 20 years, my expertise and skill is customer service and project management. Right before starting the WiseWe Company, I worked in the IT & Management Consulting Industry as a Consultant and Project Manager. I love helping people make sense out of complex variables to arrive at a solution that offers peace of mind. I got a taste of that as a consultant and in customer service but asked myself what if I could take this to another level and put honesty, integrity, love and passion first.

I started the WiseWe Company built on helping our customers have peace of mind through trust. Our customer partners know they're getting the best dedicated team who can implement and manage solutions for them. They know they're dealing with a happy, skilled customer service and project management team who is up for the task of producing whatever solution is needed from Salesforce Implementation to Social Media Management. We love what we do and I wanted to give you a few of the areas we focus on for our clients and that other growing companies should focus on. Now we're focusing on how to reach many more people and businesses, so we're creating digital products and group training programs & events. We want you to be able to get help at any time through these on-demand products.

I know you love what you do and have big goals. I'm honored to help with the information here and information I'll share through video and other upcoming books as well. Please stay in touch as we also like to share FREE PDFs and videos on important topics. Also, we'd love to invite you to our BIG conference that we're planning. Enjoy and let us know if we can help!

Find and Use Effectively the Best CRM

CRM stands for customer relationship management and businesses of all sizes need the tools and processes in place for CRM. One of the technology leaders in this space is Salesforce, however, there are other CRMs as well including HubSpot, Zoho and Microsoft. You can do a basic search to discover the leaders in the space, however that's not the point here. I want to talk more about the structure of how to use the CRM. A CRM is great at helping you manage your accounts so that you have a great view of your accounts' activities. It really serves as an end to end solution. A great CRM will allow you to view the history of client communication, current communication, current projects or tasks and other elements related to your accounts. This is really accomplished largely through the helpdesk environment that you set up through your CRM. If we take Salesforce as an example, you can not only set up a support address through your email accounts as many normally do. More importantly, you can link your support address to your CRM, and respond & track everything from just the CRM.

Besides account management and email management, the biggest thing that you're able to do is case management. With case management, all of your emails become cases and you can view and track them in a more organized manner that includes queues for your different departments. You also can assign and reassign your staff to cases and talk internally about the cases, outside of email. Imagine significantly cutting down on the emails needed to send other team members and linking chat messages to actual work and not have it be a separate entity from your work. These are not actions that can be fulfilled through a simple helpdesk email address.

There are other products besides a CRM, like Zendesk that you can use for your helpdesk but remember that Salesforce is not only a CRM but the helpdesk and it also integrates with Zendesk. Before you get too concerned about the cost of an implementation consultant partner, consider Salesforce's premier services which give you a year's worth of service from Salesforce experts so you simply need to know what you want and be able to explain it to Salesforce. The staff will then configure your Salesforce instance for you. Now, full disclosure is that their staff doesn't do everything under the sun for you, however, anything that they can't do for you, they can either give you a set of instructions, walk you through how to do it or they'll recommend using a Salesforce partner or non-partner.

We are pretty far along through an implementation and Premier Services has been able to do pretty much anything that we needed them to do in order to get the main implementation to a pretty good spot.

Top CRMs include:
1. Salesforce
2. HubSpot CRM
3. Sugar CRM
4. Insightly
5. Microsoft Dynamics

CRMs can be used for:
1. Account Management
2. Prospecting and Sales
3. Manage All Emails
4. Marketing
5. Project Management
6. More...

WISEWE TIP:

Don't wait until you reach a critical point to invest in systems, infrastructure and processes for growth. Get ahead of the business growth by investigating and investing now.

Some questions to answer. If you want to connect with us for support, send us the answers to some preliminary questions so we can have a good understanding of where you are at this point in time. Answer these for your company:

1. What industry are you in and who are some of your main competitors?
2. What volume of emails do you currently experience?
3. What volume of calls do you currently experience per day?
4. Do you expect that volume to change or remain the same?
5. Is there a good business case for designing for the reception of more calls than emails? Meaning do you want to intentionally guide customers to call instead of email?
6. What functions of a CRM as described do you think you'll most likely need.

Good companies not only know how to build great products but connect with their customers in other ways as well. Salesforce is a good example of a company that understands its customer, knows how to create an experience using the product and then connecting around the product. Their Salesforce World Tour is a great annual event held in multiple locations all around the world. I've been to the ones in New York and Washington DC, it was a great event and I'm not just saying that because of the free food that they bring out throughout the day. Not even saying that because of the exclusive events held at places like the exotic car club of Manhattan with Ferrari's and Lamborghini's. If you ever had a question about one of their products, these events are great opportunities to ask any question you may have had and see a 1 on 1 demo based on your needs. They of course have larger group sessions on several topics and live stream the entire thing with videos available afterwards as well. I can appreciate a good event and why not have an in-person event where your company can connect in real life with consumers for free. What Salesforce does and you can do is create a community of value both in product and experience.

Have a Refined Customer Service Process - SLAs, Timing and More

Next, you need a customer service process so that you not only have a technology solution that includes a helpdesk. You also need a process including SLA's for how you are going to use that end to end solution. For example, you'll want to consider timing. What do you want your policy to be for how long it should take to reply to an email or phone call? Within your Salesforce, there is also a way to connect your phone calls to the application as well. When we are talking about timing, are you going to allow 15 minutes, an hour, two hours or 24 hours for your customer service agents to be able to reply to your customers? This is not entirely up to you. You must understand your customer. Now that does not mean that you need to flat out ask them how long would you like before we reply to your email or phone call. However, have a good understanding of your customer so that the SLA you choose is appropriate. Then, you'll need to have the systems and process in place to monitor, adjust and escalate as needed.

Once emails come in and phone calls for that matter, is there a standard response for certain kinds of issues and questions? If there is a standard response or process to recommend to your customer for a solution, the next question would be, is that solution and answer documented? Now for our clients, we work with them to create user guides that cover a variety of topics. Also, these user guides are video-enabled so that when a customer clicks on a topic within the user guide, they are then taken to a short explainer video. Within Salesforce, you can take things a step further and use a knowledge base which is a collection of articles that answer questions on a variety of topics. You can have an internal knowledge base for your customer service agents. Then you could have an external knowledge base for your clients. Both would allow you to share articles that you build out in the system with answers to standard and even complex questions.

Now you have your solution that includes a helpdesk and CRM. You've also worked out your general SLA and customer service process that includes timing and the providing of answers and solutions via knowledge base or user guide content. Next, you need to have in place an escalation process. What happens when either you receive a very complex answer that you do not know the answer to or what happens when you receive a suggestion from your client base as well. Especially if you are a software company, you need to have a framework set up to handle this. We recommend that if you escalate a case to an expert on the team to answer, there is a way to communicate with your end to end solution or helpdesk environment. The idea is not to use Salesforce for your clients and then email with your team. Features like chatter within Salesforce allows you to have an internal discussion about a case a.k.a. email so that this process actually cuts down on the burden of managing a ton of emails. Other cases may turn into projects, issues or risks to initiate and track.

Repository

It's important to have a cloud-based repository for your files. You can still have your file cabinets with your paper files for anything that you need to keep a hard copy of. However, in general you'll want a cloud-based repository in case of an emergency where your hardcopy files are lost. Additionally, a repository like Box or Dropbox has other benefits such as the ability to create a filing structure so that files are easily accessible by not only yourself but the whole team as needed. With one of the systems, you can use access control to determine who can see different files and who can edit different files as well. The actual level of access control within one of these systems is comprehensive, allowing you to customize visibility and sharing of your files. Going a step even further, you're able to integrate these platforms with your CRM. For example, both Box and DropBox integrate with Salesforce allowing you to link important files to their respective accounts.

Using a repository also allows you to get further away from email especially for internal use. What this means is that instead of sending an email to one of your office colleagues with an attachment, you can share sensitive documents from Dropbox or Box. Furthermore, it makes your ability to upload to various websites like social media a lot easier. So, if you're engaged on social media like every business should be, you'll need a place to store stories, pictures and video that you'd like to use in the future. Even if you hire someone to do your social media for you and your company, you'll still want a place to be able to share files securely. The repositories that we have mentioned so far aren't necessarily for backing up all computer files. For that, you'll want to look at a few other options that allow for automatic or manual back up of files. Services like Carbonite can provide automated backup along with Norton Internet Security and a handful of others as well.

TIPS When Working from Home/Remote Work

Many companies use WebEx, GoToMeeting or a similar product. However, not many companies record the sessions that they do and create specific short or long videos for their employees and customers. If a company does record, it's usually the long form of a webinar or a session that is 1 or 2+ hours long. My recommendation here for high growth companies that have an increasing employee base is to break those 1 to 2+ hour sessions down to 3 to 5 minute videos. Once again, this is a service that we offer and provide to our clients. However, you can also do this within your company as well by recording short sessions by subject, 35 minutes long and saving as either an MP4 or WAV file. Then you can upload it to a dedicated YouTube or Vimeo site for your employees and or customers. Furthermore, this will allow you to do something that we mentioned in this book already which is the shorter videos linked to user guide topics.

Let's say by chance you don't use one of these tools with your employees or customers. Our recommendation would be to do so because getting together in person isn't always possible or convenient for employees or customers. These tools give you the ability to get together much easier. Additionally, you want to have short 30 seconds to 60 seconds videos that explain your current product as well as any new products that you're rolling out as well. These can be social media friendly videos that explain in a very simple way what your company is all about, what your biggest product is all about, what your future product is all about or where you stand on an industry important subject. Once again, if you need help producing any videos like this feel free to reach out to The WiseWe Company.

Laptop. I don't think so.

I'll admit that after working all day from home, I'd revisit that laptop after feeding the little one. As an IT consultant, one benefit (if you work for the right company) is working from home. If you don't have a large meeting or an important one to attend, you can do your work from home.
Even while writing this, my daughter wants to play with my shoes; the bottom of them at that. I'll be right back.....

Lesson: Live in the moment. Actually BE there 100%.

Give love, attention, interaction and for a little one, teaching. These things are priceless and shouldn't be overlooked.

It can be hard, especially after a long day or week to not be able to kick off your shoes or watch the television. Before the age of two, it's very likely that your child will have no interest in TV. They just want to engage with you and maybe their toys.

There's truth, simplicity and the secret to growth that lay within the way a toddler is.

We are meant to connect with each other in a meaningful way. We are meant to care for and love each other. Much of today's life is fast paced, material driven and less about love and engagement. Love is the key though. We should love the moments that we have with each other more than we love being alone with the television. Sure, we all need our time alone so I would recommend one thing when this feeling butts heads with the needs of others:

Lesson: Get out of the house and get active. Or stay in and get connected.

If you work at a desk and on the computer all day, get outside and get active with your kids or others. Think about it, you're mentally not physically fatigued. You've been typing all day not running. You may have been driving, not sprinting so we can always expend some physical energy.

If you really want to stay in, identify some activities that you can do to connect with others. Take this time to write a list.

This goes for everyone when they are around loved ones and friends. Put away those cell phones, stop the texting and engage.

Throughout this book, I've covered some of the lessons, steps, tools and more that helped me to break free from fear and doubt, to WIN@LIFE. Only you can define what it means to win but generally we could probably agree on a few points.

Remember this book talks about how I went from having no prospect or idea on how I would achieve success in life. At the time, so many negative things had happened the summer before trying to go off to college, that it carried over to college where I didn't have the right mindset to win.

- Preparing for City Track Championships where scouts were coming to see me run to determine my college scholarship qualifications
- Getting hurt in gym class of all places and not being able to

perform in the City Championships. Dream of College sports and Olympics temporarily crushed.

- No clear path or goals

I went from confusion and having no prospect of success to laser focused clarity and accomplishing my goals. The lessons, steps, tools and other information shared here was a product or integral part of the journey that I wanted to share with you. I hope that this book inspired you to achieve your goals as an entrepreneur or something else. Whatever it is, be true to yourself, go after what you truly want and do it with the highest sense of morals, ethics, values, passion and love (all of the good stuff ☺)

To:

- Clear Path and Goals
- Journey
    o Living in South Beach
    o Starting my first business
    o Finding Love
    o Graduating with an MBA, specializing in entrepreneurship
    o Having my first child – A girl
    o Living in Miami again
    o Leaving my job
    o Starting my third business/ A profitable successful venture
- Growing as a man, father, son, citizen and more.

As I finished writing this book and started to edit, I thought what better place to go and edit the book then where the entrepreneurial journey started, Miami. I decide to make a couple of visits, each a week long and stayed in South Beach, Sunny Isle Beach, Coconut Grove, downtown Brickell and Homestead. As I'm in each of these places, especially South Beach and downtown Brickell, it's a reminder of how time keeps moving and things change. New buildings were being built in both places, reminding me of this change. Whatever it is you're thinking of starting, start it now! If you don't, time will still move along. Worried about how you'll start, then start with as little risk as possible. Minimize your risk, but seriously consider starting now and use some of the lessons, stories and information in this book to help. Also reach out to us for other products, services and events that we offer so they can be helpful too.

At the same time many things stay the same. The beach is still the beach, a great place to go walk, run and eat. Of course you have to know where to go so you just don't get that typical tourist experience. That's why for one of my next books, I'll be partnering with a friend of mine to write about this and other cities giving you great travel tips.

Never Stop Celebration of Life

There are so many lessons, stories and information I share in this book that I wanted to just end on a very simple note. As I'm wrapping this book up, I'm planning to head back to New York City for a few events. One is that Caribbean Tourism event that I went to years before with my family. Now the event is in New York this year and we're going with a pretty large group. I'll be sure to share pictures and video online so be sure to connect with me there. One thing I love about NYC is the constant energy of the city, almost like a feeling of constant striving. It's like the land of goals and making things happen. Make sure wherever you are, set those goals as big as you can imagine and then make it happen every day!

ABOUT THE AUTHOR

Wayne Walsh is a creative entrepreneurial leader who has started several businesses. Before becoming an entrepreneur, Wayne worked in different industries and disciplines including retail sales, financial services, project management, IT Consulting and business operations, sharpening his customer service, management and leadership skills. Wayne earned an MBA specializing in entrepreneurship and uses his knowledge, experience and skills to help other entrepreneurs and growing businesses.

Wayne grew up in Baltimore, Maryland in the 1980s and was exposed to a rich culture of arts, music, history and more. He grew up in a loving, supportive and even competitive family of 7 where he was nurtured and challenged. Wayne's parents placed an emphasis on education and in doing so showed him the importance and power of the use of knowledge. Wayne was well travelled as a child visiting the Caribbean, being exposed to beautiful and rich culture and environment.

As an athlete, Wayne challenged himself physically and mentally winning championships with his teammates. He was able to take that same passion, love and discipline to the world of entrepreneurship to continually learn and apply more and more. He has overcome challenges in life and experienced great success personally and professionally. Wayne wants you to Win@Life!

www.ingramcontent.com/pod-product-compliance
Lightning Source LLC
Chambersburg PA
CBHW071521200326
41519CB00019B/6026